Praise for When Losses Become Legacies

"Brunke and Cowan have dared to engage our souls at the place where believers and doubters meet at the same agonizing intersection—suffering. Their writing urges us to look for the irreplaceable presence of Jesus on the difficult journey we each will eventually walk through in our seasons of personal pain and loss. Their words and stories are compelling and filled with hope as we find our footing on the solid rock."

—**Tim Simpson**, pastor of congregational care, Greenridge Baptist Church, Boyds, Maryland, and former president of the Baptist Convention of Maryland/Delaware

"Each of us is called to steward time, faith, blessings, and sorrow. The personal and heartfelt testimonies in *When Losses Become Legacies* beautifully exemplify how to turn ashes into beauty on the difficult paths each of us must walk. Through poignant stories and steady reliance on God, readers will see how to let their lights shine in the darkness for the illumination of all."

—**Sandra Byrd**, bestselling, award-winning author of *The One Year Experiencing God's Love Devotional*

"Brunke and Cowan invite us to journey with them, bearing witness to grief and loss they have known. The testimonies are beautiful and sorrowful, inspirational and encouraging. Their losses—legacies—are built on a great 'cloud of witnesses,' spurring us to run the race life sets before us. Ultimately, Brunke and Cowan bring readers the lasting hope and comfort of the Holy Spirit."

—**Nive Christodoss**, licensed clinical professional counselor and certified clinical trauma professional

"Written from the pens of tender hearts that wisely seek to redeem every loss in the light of eternal hope found only in Jesus Christ. I recommend this book to anyone who is seeking hope in what may feel like a hopeless situation."

—**Dr. John C. Palmieri**, pastor and coach at New Life Community Church, Chicago

"While reading this book, a Bible passage came to me over and over: *A word fitly spoken is like apples of gold in settings of silver* (Prov. 25:11 NKJV). The sensitivity and wisdom Brunke and Cowan bring to this jewel box of a book do indeed set gold in silver. Through true-life stories ranging from postpartum depression to grief associated with the loss of a relationship, a loved one, a dream, and beyond, these authors weave the silver and gold of hope and healing through Jesus Christ into otherwise dark and dismal landscapes. I recommend this book to anyone who has found themselves in a dark valley and in need of light."

—**Linda Brooks Davis**, award-winning author of *The Calling of Ella McFarland*

"Brunke and Cowan guide readers through a deep labyrinth of life's grief and gloom, up toward a horizon of hope—Jesus' empty tomb. *When Losses Become Legacies* offers a touching anthology of tragedies, delivering a peace that passes understanding."

—**Eric T. Eichinger**, senior pastor of Bethel Lutheran Church, Clearwater, Florida, and award-winning author of *The Final Race* and *Lord of Legends: Jesus' Redemption Quest*

"Do you remember a moment in life where it seemed that you couldn't breathe, that the hurt was overwhelming, when the emotional pain was strikingly real? Most of us tend to hide in those moments, and perhaps hide from those moments for the rest of our lives. Kristina Cowan and Christy Brunke explore those areas we try to avoid in *When Losses Become Legacies*. Through their gentle and kind-spirited authorship, they reveal in seasons of loss how God brings to life things that are hidden. A type of resurrection awaits you in these pages."

—**Dr. Mollie Bond**, professor, nonprofit professional, and author of *Hopelessly Hopeful During Separation*

When Losses Become Legacies

When Losses Become Legacies

Memoirs on Grief, God, and Glory

Christy Brunke & Kristina Cowan

Redemptive Edge
Press

Redemptive Edge Press
Monrovia, MD
redemptiveedgepress.com

When Losses Become Legacies: Memoirs on Grief, God, and Glory
First edition

Requests for information should be sent to:

- christy@redemptiveedgepress.com
- kristina@redemptiveedgepress.com

Library of Congress Control Number: 2022900288

ISBN: 979-8-9854841-8-2

Scripture is taken from *The Holy Bible: New International Version* (NIV). Copyright 1995 by Zondervan. All rights reserved.

Book cover design by Melissa Williams Design
Developmental editing by Christy Brunke and Kristina Cowan
Copy editing by Thomas Wayne Carter
Interior formatting by Christy Brunke and Kristina Cowan

*Dedicated to everyone
who has allowed the Lord
to turn their losses into legacies.*

"As the rain hides the stars, as the autumn mist hides the hills, as the clouds veil the blue of the sky, so the dark happenings of my lot hide the shining of your face from me. Yet, if I may hold your hand in the darkness, it is enough."

—Gaelic prayer, tr. Alistair MacLean

CONTENTS

Part One: Mourning

Part Two: Memories

Part Three: Miracles

Introduction

Christy Brunke

O n the stage of life, suffering invariably enters, often donning the costume we call loss. Loss of health. Loss of a marriage. Loss of a loved one.

If we let it, suffering ushers us closer to our Savior. The fleeting pain has the power to bestow an enduring reward: legacy.

As Paul said in 2 Corinthians 4:17, "For our light and momentary troubles are achieving for us an eternal glory that far outweighs them all."

In this life or the next, the Lord will restore. "And the God of all grace, who called you to his eternal glory in Christ, after you have suffered a little while, will himself restore you and make you strong, firm and steadfast" (1 Pet. 5:10).

The suffering and the restoration both have their place in our stories. After all, Jesus, in whose footsteps we seek to follow, endured the cross "for the joy set before him" (Heb. 12:2).

In Good Company

God the Son knew suffering, perhaps better than any of us ever will. Slander. Betrayal. Flogging. Crucifixion.

Before that, he knew the grief of losing a loved one, just as we inevitably do. When his friend Lazarus died, Jesus wept, even as he knew they would soon be reunited. Whether our separation from our loved ones ends quickly or tarries, grieving is good. But, as believers, we have this hope: Our grieving will one day end in a joyful reunion.

> Brothers and sisters, we do not want you to be uninformed about those who sleep in death, so that you do not grieve like the rest of mankind, who have no hope. For we believe that Jesus died and rose again, and so we believe that God will bring with Jesus those who have fallen asleep in him. (1 Thess. 4:13)

We also know this hope: No matter what kind of suffering we may endure, the Lord will never leave us. "When you pass through the waters, I will be with you; and when you pass through the rivers, they will not sweep over you. When you walk through the fire, you will not be burned; the flames will not set you ablaze" (Isa. 43:2).

In our suffering, we are surrounded by the saints, those still here and those who have gone before (Heb. 12:1). The stories of some of these saints are in this anthology. The real-life characters both entertain and inspire:

- a miniature donkey and his eccentric owner who could star in a children's picture book;
- a middle-aged divorcée who answers God's call to China and becomes a famous teacher; and
- a missions-minded contractor who encounters God before his surgery and is miraculously healed.

Miracles and Mysteries

You will see that God still performs miracles. Sometimes it's a complete physical healing. Sometimes it's a vision of God or heaven. Sometimes it's a smaller miracle of a few more days.

Often, for whatever reason, he does not. A young woman dies, leaving behind a husband and two small children. A beloved friend, parent, or grandparent passes before you're ready. At fifteen, you lose your mom to breast cancer; at thirty-nine, you lose your brother to suicide.

That fifteen-year-old, now forty-eight, is my friend and co-author, Kristina Cowan. We first met in Chicagoland in April 2011. At the time, we were both pregnant; I with my first child and she with her second. I was an aspiring writer penning my first novel. She was a seasoned journalist writing her first nonfiction book.

Along with other writers, we gathered at a Panera Bread for the inaugural meeting of a critique group. With the aroma of baked goods in the air, we founded a new chapter of Word Weavers International. Kristina was the president. I was a newbie.

Fast-forward four months. Our daughters—though due two weeks apart—were born on the same day.

The Birth of This Book

Four years later, our family moved to Maryland. Unbeknownst to me, I contracted Lyme disease. That year, my novel—which Kristina helped edit—was released. *Library Journal* named *Snow Out of Season* the Christian Fiction Debut of the Month. Soon, it topped Amazon bestseller lists in two categories.

The next year, Kristina's book—*When Postpartum Packs a Punch*—hit the shelves with praise from *Publishers Weekly*. She continued to freelance while she wrote the book, her work gracing publications like the *Ladders*, *The Huffington Post*, and Chicago's *Daily Herald*.

In 2018, after being out of touch for a while, Kristina emailed me. She was brainstorming her first novel and wondered if I'd like to meet over the phone once a month.

Meanwhile, I was outlining my first nonfiction book, a memoir about my battle with Lyme. The timing couldn't have been more perfect.

As we helped each other with our longer works, we realized we also had shorter pieces we felt compelled to share. Kristina suggested we team up to write an anthology of narrative nonfiction. So began the book you are holding in your hands or reading on a tablet.

Love, Loss, and Legacy

Losing her mom as a child, her dad more recently, and her brother to suicide, Kristina Cowan is no stranger to grief. As a pastor's wife, former missionary, and one-time seminary student, I am no stranger to God and his glory. Together we wrote these memoirs on grief, God, and glory.

This book is not an abstract theological treatise on the causes and purposes of suffering. Neither is it a psychology-based guide to grief or a compilation of fictional tales. Rather, it's a collection of true stories, creatively told, about love, loss, and legacy.

Mother loss is a gate through which almost all of us will pass. The younger the mother is when she dies, the more traumatic the experience. Our first two stories tackle this rite of passage. One is told from the perspective of a child, now grown. The other, from the perspective of a young mother.

Join us on these and seven other journeys. The cloud of witnesses is cheering you on.

Part One: Mourning

"And there is a similar distinction between the two ideas of death, between the two types of tragedy. There is the tragedy that is founded on the worthlessness of life; and there is the deeper tragedy that is founded on the worth of it. The one sort of sadness says that life is so short that it can hardly matter; the other that life is so short it matters forever."

—G. K. Chesterton
The Illustrated London News, June 4, 1910

Chapter One

My Mother, Myself: Growing Older Than She Lived to Be

Kristina Cowan

I 'm strapped to a hospital bed as a doctor looms over my left eyebrow, stitching it with a needle. The rush of blood spouting from my face slows to a trickle. I squeeze my dad's hand. My entire fist wraps around one of his fingers. In the distance, my mom crouches and sobs. My dad's strong, warm hand is my anchor.

The bleeding stops.

The doctor's gentle pressure lifts.

My mom eases into silence.

I'm okay.

This is my first memory of being alive. I was just over a year old. My parents had left me with a babysitter for the first time, only to dart home after I careened into a glass coffee table, splitting my forehead with a gash that nearly razed my left eye.

"She's lucky," the doctor had said, according to my dad's retelling. "Another millimeter, and she would've lost that eye."

My mom later told me she couldn't bear being near the doctor when he pierced my head with the needle. Seeing her baby's blood-soaked face had sapped her trauma tolerance. She asked my dad to stand with me as she watched from afar.

Fourteen years later, my mom died from breast cancer. My dad would be my primary parent for the next thirty years.

In 2020, as I turned forty-six—the same age my mom was when she died—I wondered whether that initial memory was a foreshadowing. My mom has been mostly a mystery-parent, dwelling in the shadows. My dad was the dominant one, on hand for all of my life's big moments.

I have many unanswered questions for and about my mom. I was too young when I lost her to consider asking her big questions. I have no sense of what an adult relationship with a mother is like. What I miss most is her not being here to embrace and influence my two children.

I have few unanswered questions about my dad. I had enough time with him to ask all of my questions—to understand his history, his views, and the parts of him that are alive in me. As I move through life, I hear his voice of reason. He embraced my children, and I know they'll not forget his influence.

My parents in the 1980s

Growing older than a parent who died is a bag of mixed emotions. Psychologist Ryan Howes says it might be "enlightening, debilitating, even paralyzing."

Maxine Harris, author of the book, *The Loss That Is Forever: The Lifelong Impact of the Early Death of a Mother or Father*, says this passage is often anxiety-filled. "The age at which a mother or father died serves as a milestone that many fear will mark the end of their own journey," she writes.[1]

Bypassing my mom's age was, in fact, fraught. One of my goals is inextricably linked with my children: a home warmed by the love and support of a mother and a father. It's one of the greatest advantages my husband and I can give them, and I go to lengths to protect it.

Because my mom died of breast cancer before she reached menopause, I started mammograms in my late twenties. When I turned forty, one revealed precancerous breast cells. After months of biopsies and advanced testing, I opted for a preventative double-mastectomy.

Within the next five years, my chance of developing breast cancer was more than one in two. I was proactive because my mom wasn't. For a year, she ignored a ballooning lump. When she finally sought a doctor, the lump dwarfed a tennis ball. It was a rare form of inoperable breast cancer. She died about a year after her diagnosis.

My mom was known for being late to work and tardy for family gatherings. Since she drove well under the speed limit, a policeman once pulled her over for driving too slowly. She was unhurried about everything, including her health. If it was meant to be, she said, God would heal her from cancer. If not, she reveled in the heavenly home awaiting her. The other half of her inaction was fear. She didn't want to know what the lump was.

Falling on my teenage ears, these explanations struck me as irresponsible for a mother of three. They still do. I learned from that experience and sought to do better for my children.

When my mom died, I felt as if I had almost lost one of my eyes again. The familiar world melted into a blur. My mom was away, but my dad remained. Regaining my focus took time. My perspective was forever altered. And though losing a parent early in life isn't something I would wish for anyone, it has been, in many ways, an uncommon gift.

A Thanaversary in 2020

Howes has coined a term for the milestone of reaching the age a parent was at their death: a thanaversary. He explains it in *Psychology Today*:

> In Greek mythology, Thanatos was the personification of death. Psychology, philosophy, medicine, and other disciplines call their study of death, dying, grief, and sociological attitudes toward death 'thanatology.' So thanatos fits, some sort of -versary makes sense, therefore I present: 'Thanaversary.' It's a little dark, but I think it

represents both the bitter and sweet of a day like this.[2]

My thanaversary landed in 2020. I knew it would be a pivotal year in my world. I didn't know the whole world would spin out of control. The drumbeat of 2020 sounded global upheaval. From the pandemic to social unrest to political turmoil, daily life was framed by peril. It's not by chance that my thanaversary surfaced as the world unraveled. It's by God's design.

In the thirty-two years since my mom died, I have thought about grief and loss. They have become, as author Hope Edelman suggests in *Motherless Daughters*, my legacy.[3] I've learned to weave them into my life in healthy, meaningful ways. Doing so has been practical, in part—I also lost my brother to suicide in 2013.

When we face monumental, traumatic losses, the road forks. We can strike out into the darkness, or we can chase and reclaim joy. The gospel calls believers in Christ to the second path, where we repurpose our pain to help others:

> Praise be to the God and Father of our Lord Jesus Christ, the Father of compassion and the God of all comfort, who comforts us in all our troubles, so that we can comfort those in any trouble with the comfort we ourselves receive from God. For just as we share abundantly in

the sufferings of Christ, so also our comfort
abounds through Christ. (2 Cor. 1:3-5)

Extending Comfort

Through my writing, I have sought to comfort others who
have experienced significant grief and loss. In 2020, with
the pandemic afflicting people from all walks of life, I was
reminded to keep extending that comfort.

Millions have died from COVID-19. Lockdowns have
shuttered scores of small businesses and shattered
livelihoods. Anxiety, depression, trauma, substance abuse,
and suicide are all on the rise, along with crime. Too many
people have been isolated from friends and family, steeped
in loneliness, melancholy, and rage.

We would rather ignore these harsh realities, especially
death. Isn't happiness our destiny? As Aleksandr
Solzhenitsyn pointed out, it's not: "If humanism were right
in declaring that man is born only to be happy, he would not
be born to die. Since his body is doomed to die, his task on
earth evidently must be of a more spiritual nature."[4]

Death is scary. If it weren't, I wouldn't write about my
thanaversary. It would be just another day.

If I were to die when my children are young, my
history—that of the motherless child—would repeat for
them. But I'm not in control.

My task on earth isn't to be afraid of what I can't control. The Bible tells us this more than once. Isaiah 41:10 is a good example: "So do not fear, for I am with you; do not be dismayed, for I am your God. I will strengthen you and help you; I will uphold you with my righteous right hand."

Struggles are gritty passages to an infinite supply of grace. One of my tasks on earth is to share this truth with others in such a way that it serves as a source of comfort and a call to action.

The Struggle as Legacy

Struggles are humbling and uncomfortable. If we allow them to be, they're gentle nudges—and sometimes, necessarily forceful shoves—back to the Cross, the consummate point of grace. At the foot of the Cross, fear and control lose their grip on us.

Here, we reckon with our belief that Jesus Christ weathered the ultimate struggle with evil, conquered death, and regained his life in its final, glorified form. By sacrificing everything, he unlocked his legacy, our free and unearned inheritance. This means we have the freedom to sacrifice, develop a spirit of overcoming, and regain our lives on the other side of eternity.

Through struggles, we live out Christ's legacy. He grants them to refine our character. Romans 5:3-4 reminds us, "we also glory in our sufferings, because we know that suffering produces perseverance; perseverance, character; and character, hope."

To human ears, "hardship as the wellspring of hope" has a counterintuitive ring. Words fail to fully explain how it's true. But it is. Human character won't improve without friction, without grit.

Bethany Williamson, associate professor of English at Biola University, writes: "No one, in their right mind and earthly body, can bear the glorious, penetrating, blinding light of divine Presence without coming undone. We rightly desire purity, but we also recognize that purification requires pain."[5]

Sorrow's Blinding Splendor

If we are to accept struggle as part of the human condition, we need to reframe our view. Nicholas Wolterstorff, an author and retired Yale theology professor who lost his son in a mountain-climbing accident, has written about this:

> God is not only the God of the sufferers but the God who suffers. The pain and fallenness of humanity have entered into his heart. Through the prism of my tears I have seen a suffering God. It is said of God that no one can behold his face and live. I always thought this meant that no one could see his splendor and live.

A friend said perhaps it meant that no one could see his sorrow and live. Or perhaps his sorrow is splendor. And great mystery: to redeem our brokenness and lovelessness the God who suffers with us did not strike some mighty blow of power but sent his beloved son to suffer *like* us, through his suffering to redeem us from suffering and evil. Instead of explaining our suffering God shares it.[6]

Wolterstorff's words bring comfort and clarity. When I see suffering through these rightful lenses, it takes the shape of a gift.

Whether I live or not, my children will face struggles. They will suffer at some point. I pray that they'll draw closer to Christ through all of it and learn to see the experiences as veiled gifts.

Likewise, God can use our current global struggles to achieve his plan, which is always flawless, in the end. He does that through his followers, his hands and feet in the mortal realm.

Life is an ebbing, flowing, changing current of struggles. May God grant us courage to be his hands and feet as we rise to meet the path ahead. May the journey be one of grace and grit, ever refining us.

The Abiding Anchor

When you lose someone close, especially early in life, finding the upsides is challenging—and redemptive.

Losing my mom has proven to be one of the strongest influencers of my attitude and my actions as a woman, a wife, and a mother. It has shaped me in ways I can see, and in ways I cannot. Most importantly, being a motherless daughter for most of my life has pointed me time and again to my faith in Christ.

Maxine Harris writes, "Thirty, forty, or fifty years after the death occurred, men and women still refer to the early death of a parent as the defining event of their lives."[7]

What I remember most about my mom are three things: her unwavering faith in Christ, her willingness to share it with anyone—everyone, really—and her overcoming spirit.

Well before she fell ill, she would tell me, "I'll die someday. Your dad will die one day. People will let you down, leave you behind. The one person who won't leave you, and who loves you more than your dad and I do, is Jesus Christ. Seek him with all that you have, for your whole life, and you won't go wrong."

These conversations transpired when I was quite young. My emotional landscape was undeveloped; my faith, immature. I thought she was overstating her case.

My dad, a first-generation Greek American raised in the Orthodox church, was embarrassed by her zealous approach.

He said "beating people over the head with the Bible" would alienate them. Faith, he said, was a personal journey best kept to ourselves.

Taking a cue from my dad, I ducked for cover—literally and figuratively—when my mom witnessed in public. I worried what people would think of her, of me. Life since my mom has softened me some.

When I encountered postpartum depression after my first child was born—spurred in part because of my mom's absence—the darkness seemed absolute. My faith in Christ delivered me from it. Several years later, my brother's suicide was devastating. Apart from my faith, the grief would be stifling. Finding redemption would be impossible.

These trials have made me more willing to share my faith. I did so publicly in my debut book. It was a stretch. As a classically schooled journalist, I was trained not to mention two things: faith and politics.

I left the breaking-news business years ago. I still believe it's not the place to share your faith or your politics. But the writing I do now affords me the opportunity to discuss the former.

My mom's faith was her anchor. The storms in her life didn't cease. But her anchor abided. Though she witnessed through words, most striking was the witness of her actions. They were marked by uncommon forgiveness, humility, and a penitent heart. That indelible impression of her reminds me that dropping the anchor of faith is a daily endeavor.

Mom in Medina, Ohio, circa 1985

Dads and Motherless Daughters

A mother's death carves an immense chasm into a child's life, one that cannot—and should not—be filled. Leaving a rightful space for her memory is healthy. A child can mind the gap in productive ways, with the help of a strong surviving parent, or other adults who serve as mentors.

I had my dad for forty-four years. It made all the difference. He raised me to seek first an education, to work hard, and to be self-sufficient. He employed a sterling work ethic.

Raised by immigrant parents, he navigated both Greek and American cultures. Greek was his first language until kindergarten. Often chided for his accent and last name, he learned to hide his accent and speak Greek only when necessary. Much later, he traded our last name—Leakos—for an Americanized one. Minor tradeoffs, he called them, in exchange for the many freedoms his family had found in the United States.

Dad's example has translated into a lifetime of good things for me. My work ethic is his.

When I was accepted into Northwestern University, he supported my undergrad work, and later, championed my return as a graduate student. When my first book was released, he bought two copies: one to preserve, unopened, and another to read. When *Publishers Weekly* applauded it,[8] Dad echoed:

> I read your new book review. I am so glad for you. The praise that you received tells you that you have done a great job and gives you satisfaction to know that you have the skill to go on. And if writing more books is what you choose to do, you have the skill and knowledge to do so. I am very proud of you.[9]

The bond I had with my dad meant I didn't gather my identity from romantic relationships. Psychology tells us that a girl's early attachment patterns to her dad shape her relationships later in life.[10] I didn't grow up thinking marriage would round out my world or perfect my life. When I did find the man I would marry, the right reasons motivated me.

Had my mom lived, I may have reaped these benefits just the same. It's impossible to surmise. I am certain, though, that my connection with my dad was strengthened because he had long served as a sole parent.

An Upside of Early Loss

When you lose something physically vital at a young age—for example, your eyesight—research shows that something else gets stronger, such as your hearing.[11] The same is true when you lose a fundamental pillar of your emotional health, like a mother. You get emotionally stronger in other areas.

Without my mom's protection, my independence and resolve sharpened. For better and worse, that sharpening has persisted. These qualities are helpful for meeting worldly demands posed by careers, deadlines, and to-do lists. They can also be sticking points. Hope Edelman writes:

> One out of three motherless women who could identify a positive effect of their early losses named 'independence' and 'self-reliance,' often

citing these as their passports to professional success. You don't have to lose a mother to become an independent woman, but there's often a strong relationship between the two.[12]

Independent is defined as "not subject to control by others: self-governing," or "not looking to others for one's opinions or for guidance in conduct."[13]

My independent streak has served especially well in my work. Hatching ideas for books and stories, meeting deadlines, and working for myself come naturally. I've been more successful without a boss. It also has helped me to think for myself and resist cultural pushes for conformity. Independent thinking, often in short supply, is a hallmark of American individualism and a facet of our God-given free wills.

There's a downside to independence: asking for help. We motherless daughters prefer to do things ourselves. But going it alone sometimes renders us stuck in reverse. Insight from others sheds the light we need to move forward.

Resolve

Soon after my mom died, my dad suggested that I might be distracted by grief.

"It's okay if your grades slip a little," he said.

I shuddered. I was used to straight-A report cards.

"My grades will not slip," I said.

I buried myself in my studies. That resolve helped me get into college and graduate school, work as a journalist in two major cities, and confront postpartum depression. It has evolved into a reflex: the spirit of the overcomer.

Most of the men and women Harris interviewed point to a similar tendency. She writes:

> If they had been given a choice, they would have selected to grow up with the support and encouragement of two loving parents. Yet many likened their experience to the child who is taught to swim by being thrown into the lake. One has no choice. If you want to survive, you learn to swim.[14]

Survival for the motherless or fatherless child hinges on keen determination. Yet it has a downside. My resolve at times hardens into rigidity. I like things to go according to my plan. For the believer in Christ, this is problematic. Scripture reminds us that our plans aren't supposed to be sovereign.

Isaiah 55:8 says, "'For my thoughts are not your thoughts, neither are your ways my ways,' declares the Lord."

Proverbs 19:21 says, "Many are the plans in a person's heart, but it is the Lord's purpose that prevails."

And Jeremiah 10:23 says, "Lord, I know that people's lives are not their own; it is not for them to direct their steps."

Letting go—of plans, people, ideas—is difficult. It's tricky to release control while serving as the hands and feet of Christ. I get it wrong more than I get it right. The best guides are the Bible and prayer. When I spend more time in both, I gain an otherworldly edge that furnishes me with a wisdom unmatched by even the healthiest versions of independence and resolve.

Grit and Grace

Mother's Day 2019, in Chicago

Mother loss, motherhood, and writing—I often lean on this trifecta for my identity. But not one of them defines me.

My identity, in good times and bad, is found only in Christ. Some of my identifying parts are indeed the struggles of mother loss, the gift of motherhood, and the challenges of being a writer. But they aren't the whole. Christ is meant to be our whole.

The phrase "identity in Christ" is one Christ-followers kick around. How do we reach that high ground? To be fair, it's an elusive goal. There's no direct path. And I don't think we arrive this side of eternity. It's a moving target, and life is the chase. Praying and reading our Bibles—these are God-given roadmaps. Author Ann Voskamp writes:

> In tumultuous times, there is only One Voice that can calm seas. And I keep reaching first thing every morning for His Word. Because? When the sun comes to the window every morning, it comes on fire with a message it can't contain: The One who is the Word wants to have a word with you. To neglect the only Voice that calms waves is to invite internal chaos. Because honestly, and with great tenderness: One day, either this world is going to blow apart, or your own world is going to blow apart—and the only way to survive is to keep setting apart time now to let God's Spirit blow in. Jesus loves us and this I know: Apathy for God's Word leads to atrophy of a soul. Knowing

God's Word is the only way to know your own face. Who we are is only found in the home of him.[15]

In the home of him, I rest knowing mother loss is part of the gritty grace God has allowed into my life. I'm thankful I lived to see my thanaversary, and that it fell in 2020. These are steps along the path of my earthly walk, the prelude to my eternal life story.

Chapter Two

Pepper's Very Bad Day: Rebecca Pedroza's Story

Christy Brunke

Have you ever had a bad day? A really bad day? Have you looked back later and decided it was ultimately a good day?

Pepper's Good & Bad Day by Marci McGill is a classic children's book that my mom read to my brothers and me many times. The normally cheerful Pepper possum wakes up grumpy because he lost his favorite hat. Then, everything seems to go wrong. By bedtime, he recovers his hat and realizes it was a good day, after all.

Years later, I encountered a real-life Pepper: my friend Becky. In May 2006, we served in China for three weeks, teaching English at Jiangxi Normal University. While we were there, Becky faced her own bad day. Though the details are hazy now, her experience illustrated Murphy's Law: "Anything that can go wrong will go wrong."

"I'm going to call you Pepper," I said with a grin. I shared the story from *The Six Little Possums* series but misremembered the title as *Pepper's Very Bad Day*.

Laughing in her endearing way, Becky tried out the name a few times: "Pepper." After that, the day brightened. And the name stuck.

Servant Year and Starting a Family

That year, Pepper served as an intern at our church in Chicagoland. The program was called Servant Year.

Becky was uncommonly beautiful. Everything she touched was transformed as if by stardust, glittering in her wake. She dreamed up dazzling bulletin inserts and flyers for church events. She converted the dingy basement into a warm-and-inviting lounge for Saturday night services. Coffee brewed. Soft sofas beckoned. Autumn-colored fabric hung from the ceiling. Cream-shaded lamps cast a comfortable glow.

For Christmas, she decked the halls with wreaths and tastefully trimmed trees. She launched a poinsettia project, with fresh plants gracing our Advent stage. On Christmas Eve, people who paid for them in advance would carry them home. Unfortunately, Pepper forgot to water the plants, and they withered and died. With a sheepish grin, she sprang into action, determined to right her wrong. And she did. She replaced the lifeless plants with new poinsettias, no one the wiser.

While she lived with the interns, I stayed with her mom and enjoyed Becky's bedroom, elegantly decorated in stunning shades of purple.

Two years later, on my wedding day, she styled my hair, applied my makeup, and served as our wedding coordinator. Pepper was even armed with my lip gloss whenever I needed it. Thanks to her and her mom, Mariann, plus another friend, I knew no worries that day.

2012: Becky (left) with her mom and sisters

By the time Becky was thirty, she had her own charming family. She had married her high-school sweetheart, Tony, and had given birth to two children. But when Mia was five and Mateo just three, Pepper lost something much dearer than a hat.

An Unwanted Yuletide Gift

Just before Christmas 2012, Becky awoke with what felt like a bruise under her right breast. "Is this a lump," she thought, "or am I just being dramatic?"

For the next few days, she hid her discovery, not wanting to frighten her family. Still, she repeatedly inspected the area. Was it cancer?

While her mom was in town for the holidays, Becky shared the news with her and Tony. Mariann encouraged her to see a doctor. They hoped it was a mild infection that could be treated with antibiotics.

By the day of the appointment, the lump had disappeared. "Just keep an eye on it," the doctor said.

Eventually, the lump resurfaced under Becky's armpit. It was now the size of a golf ball.

"Other than the irritating bulge coming from my armpit," Becky said, "I felt perfectly fine. Yes, I had developed some night sweats, and I was a little tired. But when you're raising two rambunctious children, who isn't?"

An ultrasound revealed that Becky needed a biopsy. While she was in surgery, the doctor met with Tony. "What I removed from your wife is not good. It looks like it might be some sort of lymphoma, but we have to wait for pathology to come back."

"My wife has cancer," rolled on repeat through Tony's mind. He needed to see her, hug her, hold her. He couldn't hold back his tears.

Breast Cancer and a Blog

As they absorbed the news, Becky developed a blog called *SincerelySurrender*. "It's a place where I can be honest and real about who I am and share my love for the Lord. He walks with me every day on this journey through cancer."

After a seemingly endless month, the results arrived. Sort of. Becky appeared to have stage 3C breast cancer, but even the Mayo Clinic was unsure of its origin.

"I was scared," Tony said. "Her cancer was aggressive. The mass they found was growing rapidly and had already spread from her breast into her lymph nodes."

Becky's oncologist treated it as breast cancer and ordered chemotherapy. Before she received her port, Becky posted her third blog.

> As long as we have waited for an answer, it seems like things are happening so quickly.

Honestly, it's not that I am scared, but I feel like I am not ready for this. As a mother who is always in control of everything, now is the time to give God everything and know that he is in control.

Wiggin' Out

"In preparation for what may come," Becky got a pixie cut. She dubbed her new look "The Rock Star."

In March, she took on her first chemotherapy treatment with a smile. She wasn't scared or anxious. She felt God's peace. "He has been faithful in carrying me through this week," she wrote, "one day at a time."

The first week of April, Becky felt incredible. Her energy was higher than it had been for months. "I had to take advantage of my good days, and what better way than to wig shop?"

Becky found several wigs that matched her former style, a side-parted, shoulder-length bob. In the end, she ordered the "Kim Kardashian." The length let her hair stylist "cut and style it to our liking."

Losing your hair seems to be one of the most traumatic aspects of chemo, especially for a woman. For her kids' sake, Becky turned it into a fun event. Knowing she would soon lose her hair, she invited a friend over to shoot family photos.

Then, Becky's hair stylist buzzed her hair. Mia helped. Afterward, they took more pictures. Becky still looked gorgeous. As a relative pointed out, she eclipsed Demi Moore's G.I. Jane.

2013: Family photo before Becky's hair buzz

When Mateo saw her short hair, he dubbed her "Mommy Boy." Mariann turned toward the window and wiped away her tears.

"I Just Want to Feel Better Again"

Doctors had warned Becky that the first four chemotherapy treatments would be the worst. They weren't kidding. She endured nausea, exhaustion, bone pain, and a swollen esophagus, to name just a few downsides.

As she prepared for her third treatment, she wrestled with anxiety. "My suffering may be overwhelming, and it may feel like it will never end. But my hope is in the Lord, the God that created the heavens and the earth."

By the next month, Becky longed for chemo to end. "I just want to feel better again."

All four treatments in the first round wrapped up in May 2013. She had spent most of those eight weeks in her room, sleeping or lying in a fog. She was emotionally and spiritually drained. "While I needed the rest to recover, I could not help but feel an overwhelming amount of guilt," she wrote. "I missed my family. I felt guilty I was not taking care of them. I felt guilty for the way it was affecting them and their daily routine."

Becky wasn't done. After a two-week break, her second round of chemotherapy awaited.

Soaring Through Her Second Round

"So far, I am feeling wonderful," Becky typed, smiling. "I have energy and no physical side-effects."

Summer camp kicked off for her kids. Her mom returned home to Hawaii. "I am finally getting back into the swing of things. Most important, the kids are starting to feel a bit back to normal . . . I have to say, it feels great to be able to get up in the morning and have just a regular day."

By the next month, things were still looking up. "I have been soaring through this second round of chemo. I have three weeks left, and then I am done!" After sharing an update on future treatments, she offered her testimony.

My faith has given me a peace I cannot understand. A peace that whatever the Lord has planned—and all the unknown—will all be okay, no matter the outcome. I know his plan is perfect and far better than anything I can do on my own. God knows best. Mia will be turning six on July 20, and it is unbelievable how fast she has grown . . . Mateo has been as active as ever but has been so affectionate, always telling me how much he loves me. The sweetest words to my ears, it melts my heart every time I hear them.

In August, Becky crossed the finish line. "It has been only by the grace of God that I have successfully completed sixteen sessions of chemotherapy within eighteen weeks."

Her struggle continued. She now needed a double mastectomy.

Double Whammies

Lung, ovarian, and pancreatic cancer ran on Mariann's side of the family. Her grandparents and several uncles had already died from one of those three types of cancer. Her mother had fought colon cancer and won—with the Lord's help.

Walt, Becky's dad, had battled prostate cancer since 2002. Once Becky was diagnosed, the two were tested for a breast cancer gene mutation (BRCA). Both tested positive for an abnormal BRCA1.

Becky's risk for breast cancer had always been eighty percent. She also had a forty-percent chance of developing ovarian cancer. Removing her ovaries and breast tissue would lower her future odds for both. The removed tissue would then be tested for cancer.

"It was such a relief for us to finally arrive at the hospital for my surgery," Becky wrote. "It was a day we knew we would have to face, and it came so quickly. It was clear from the beginning that God had planned out every detail from the moment I was diagnosed until now."

Before the surgery, friends from church prayed over Becky and her family. "While I drifted off to sleep [during surgery], which was only a moment for me, my husband, parents and close family waited in anticipation."

The mastectomies took five hours. Tony paced, consumed by his fears of the outcome. Afterward, in recovery, Becky asked for her husband. She had to see him. Once reunited, they learned that the surgery went extremely well. From the naked eye, the surgeon couldn't find a mass within the removed tissue.

Two days later, as Becky prepared to go home, her oncologist called with good news. The pathology report showed that everything was negative. No trace of cancer lurked in the removed ovaries, breast tissue, or twelve lymph nodes. Becky's eyes brimmed with tears as she whispered a prayer of thanksgiving.

Radiation, and Back to Reality

In September, she waded into her first of thirty radiation treatments. By the time she completed the twelfth, her skin had turned to leather. It chafed at everything, including her clothes.

Her family hosted a fundraiser for breast cancer awareness. Becky wanted everyone to learn the value of self-advocating. "As women and busy moms, it is so easy to put yourself last. The smallest abnormality may be your biggest symptom."

Within two months, Becky finished her radiation. She celebrated. But she wasn't ready for what came next.

During treatment, those closest to Becky were unwavering in their care. Her dad took her to scans, MRIs, and chemotherapy treatments. Her mom flew back and forth from Hawaii to cook, clean, and care for her and the kids. Her husband, mother-in-law, and other friends and family served her in countless ways.

When her treatment ended, so did the help. Mariann went home to her husband. Tillie, her mother-in-law, returned to work. Tony plunged into a new schedule with his job. No longer were friends and family cleaning, cooking, or folding bottomless piles of laundry.

Becky felt like she was thrown to the wolves. Meanwhile, her children were the same, and she was, in her words, "almost eaten alive!" People still helped from time to time, but the shift from 24-7 care to full-time mom was sudden and jarring.

Though she felt well and enjoyed good days, she endured some "really bad ones too." Still, she added, "I needed this push back into reality. It's probably what is keeping me going."

Remission and Relapse

During Becky's year-long remission, her faith in God did not change. She knew he had healed and restored her. She would put the past behind her and return to normal life. In her own words:

> I wanted to just live my life with my incredible husband and my two beautiful children. I

wanted a simple, calm, comfortable lifestyle. I spent most of my time living day by day, doing the mundane tasks of life. I didn't spend much time or energy praying, reading my Bible, going to church . . . In all honesty, I was spiritually dead inside. So, as August came to an end, my one-year cancer-free diagnosis did as well.

Late in the summer of 2014, Becky was tired, sluggish, and a bit off. Blood tests revealed that her thyroid was underactive, so her doctor prescribed medicine.

On August 22, she celebrated her one-year anniversary of being cancer-free. Around the same time, she grew dizzy and felt off-balance. She assumed it was her body adjusting to the new medication.

While on vacation with her family in California, a dark suspicion brewed in Becky's mind. Following her own counsel to self-advocate, she sought more tests.

In September, she had a full body scan as well as an MRI of her brain. The results were grim. She had a limb-threatening tumor, which was causing paralysis on her left side. Worse, the two-centimeter mass was on the right side of her brain stem, an inoperable area. But it wasn't brain cancer: It was metastatic breast cancer. The cancer had advanced to stage four and spread to another vital part of Becky's body.

With Aunt Sally, who had ovarian cancer

A Tormenting Wait

Her radiation oncologist recommended CyberKnife Radioactive Therapy. Though this treatment is outpatient and non-invasive, it requires preparation to be precise. Making sure the radiation targeted only the tumor—not Becky's brain tissue—would be crucial.

Over the next fourteen days, Becky met with the doctors from her medical team.

Her younger sister, Stephanie, posted on Becky's blog. "I'm not a blogger. Far from it. What I am is a sister, a pretty scared one." She went on to describe how they had loved having their "sister, wife, mom, daughter, niece and aunt back! Most important, she was healthy. Then in the blink of an eye, she wasn't."

"The wait for radiation," Stephanie added, "while short, has been excruciating."

During those two weeks, Becky's health declined. Insomnia plagued her nights; extreme fatigue, her days. Her speech slurred, and the left side of her face drooped and went numb. Her body swelled, transforming her appearance overnight. Without help, she could not eat, walk, write, shower, or even use the bathroom.

Some symptoms stemmed from the tumor, and others were from the steroids. The result was the same: She needed constant care.

"I'm dying right before their eyes," Becky thought, along with a barrage of other sad reflections. *I don't want my children to see me this way. I'll never put my kids to bed again. Who will help Tony raise our children?*

"Jesus, Fight for Me"

"Jesus," Becky prayed, "fight for me because I am too tired to fight." Stephanie wrote:

> Although she hasn't been herself lately, one thing hasn't changed: her faith. She has not stopped trusting him. She has been so humble,

42

even joking in the most saddening situations.
She has continued to pray and trust in him . . .
It's a relief to still see that light shining inside of
her even though she is going through so much.

Outwardly, Becky wasted away. Inwardly, she was renewed. "God has awakened my soul and put a strong message on my heart to share," she told her readers.

It's time for us to wake up! Where are you at
spiritually? Are you awake or have you been
spiritually asleep, as I was? There will come a
day when we will all come face to face with
Jesus Christ. We are not promised tomorrow.
Eventually, we will all pass away. My question
for you is: Do you know where you will spend
eternity?

After sharing verses from Romans, she ended with a prayer from 1 Peter 1:8-9.

My prayer for you is that you love him even
though you have never seen him. Though you do
not see him now, you trust him; and you rejoice
with a glorious, inexpressible joy. The reward

for trusting him will be the salvation of your souls.

Five CyberKnife treatments later, Becky's mass had shrunk almost in half, to 1.2 centimeters.

Recovery and Restless Legs

For the next two months, Becky recovered. Gradually, her sleep improved. Her energy resurfaced. Even the side-effects from the high dose of steroids ebbed.

Still, the advent of the new year—2015—brought a return of her headaches and restless legs.

Her doctors prescribed medicine to ease the symptoms. Unfortunately, it kicked up other reactions like insomnia and mood swings. Becky felt like a zombie.

Another MRI revealed brain swelling in the treated section. The area was now 1.7 centimeters. Was the swelling spurred by tumor death or regrowth? Becky and her support network prayed that it was tumor death. In the meantime, they monitored her symptoms.

Her mom encouraged her: "At the top of each hour, ask the Lord to get you through that hour only. That way you are focused on only the hour. Tomorrow is not promised to any of us, so live for today."

One more MRI showed that the swelling in Becky's brain had subsided. Though the tumor appeared to be shrinking, it lingered. Becky's team of doctors weaned her off the steroids and began chemotherapy.

A Memorable Summer

"With this next stage, I can't help but feel like I'm running out of time. My faith has not changed, my trust in my Savior has not changed. But I feel the need to make the most memorable moments with my family right now."

Over the next five months, Becky paused her blogging. She finished chemotherapy and spent an unforgettable summer with her little loves. As she said, "Things were smoothing out again and finally feeling like normal."

They celebrated milestones. Mia turned eight, Tony turned thirty-three, and Becky's grandma turned ninety.

June 2015: Mariann's sixtieth birthday

"The kids took karate . . . and hated it," Becky said. "Mia started third grade, and I made it to see Mateo start kindergarten! We even went on our first mini-family-trip to Wisconsin Dells."

Two follow-up MRIs indicated that the brain tumor had diminished. What was once 2.2 centimeters was now only 6 millimeters. To boot, there was no swelling. The future looked promising.

Changing Winds and a Wedding

A November MRI bore bad news. At 14 millimeters, the tumor had more than doubled in size since September. Becky wrote:

> Now, that may seem so tiny, so harmless. But that is not the case. The tiniest thing can bring so much destruction. It is not only aggressive, but it is in a very fragile and dangerous spot. I will continue to keep my eyes and heart on him, my God, my Savior, my everlasting Father. For he keeps me in perfect peace, and I will trust him forever.

She began her third round of chemo with hopes it would be as effective as it was the previous year.

On December 10, 2015, she and Tony renewed their vows at Dunne Park, near a wooden bridge and a shimmering lake. With the weather a brisk forty-nine degrees, they and the kids donned black jackets. A grinning Mateo darted from the gazebo across the grass. Mia's giggles echoed after him like the sound of frolicking fairies.

During the ceremony, the couple held hands, Becky's white blouse rippling in the wind. At the end, Tony's arms shot high in celebration, his face radiant. Becky, her face upturned to heaven, whispered, "Thank you."

Afterward, as darkness descended, foreshadowing the future, Christmas lights twinkled around them. No matter what was to come, Emmanuel, along with his saints and angels, would abide.

Renewal of vows on December 10, 2015

Four Brain Surgeries

Laser ablation surgery at the University of Chicago was the doctors' final attempt to kill Becky's tumor. Their aim was to stop her tremors and paralysis.

The surgeons originally thought the procedure a success. Later, they discovered that a marginal amount of the tumor remained.

After Becky's rehabilitation at a medical center, her family was elated to bring her home. Their joy, though, was short-lived.

The next month, Becky began vomiting. She landed back in the hospital, diagnosed with hydrocephalus. Fluid had built up in her brain. To release the fluid, surgeons performed an external ventricular drain (EVD).

Becky went home in early June, but two days later, she blacked out. An ambulance rushed her back to the University of Chicago Medical Center.

This time, doctors determined that she had a brain infection. They immediately removed the EVD catheter and replaced it with a temporary drain.

With the infection cleared by late June, Becky had her fourth brain surgery within two-and-a-half months. This time, surgeons inserted a shunt to drain the remaining fluid from the infection. All went well.

Continued Rehab Denied

Becky transferred back to Resurrection Medical Center for rehab. Unable to use her left side, she struggled to swallow liquids, unless they were thickened. Bright lights agitated her. Keeping her right eye open was challenging. She needed help with almost everything.

She headed into chemo treatments. Again.

Doctors removed the staples from her brain.

On July 9, she met with the doctors and therapists from her rehabilitation team. She would continue rehab through month's end. If she preferred, she could stay indefinitely.

That day, Becky hit a speed bump. The insurance company wanted to discharge her by July 14. Becky pleaded her case, and an insurance representative met with her the next day.

"The visit was intense—lots of yelling and arguing," Stephanie told Becky's readers. "They say she's not improving. They won't give any other reason for denying it. They approved her to stay until Monday and will re-assess then."

Braving the Final Battle

In mid-July, Becky went home. She longed to be with her family. She had exhausted all treatment options but one: the chemo pill.

During a conference call with her oncologists, both told her it would not eliminate her tumor. Though it might stunt its growth, it could also make her severely ill. In fact, she might never recover from such a serious illness. Even if it worked, she could only take it for two months. Both doctors told her she did not need to take the chemo pill.

Regardless, she would try it. She fought as hard as she could to stay alive as long as she could—despite her personal pain—for her family. She didn't want to leave her children motherless and her husband a widower.

"People can look at a hero as a person who saves someone's life out of a burning car," Tony said. "But my wife is a hero every day."

"I want my kids to know what love is through the way I love their mom," he added. "I want our kids to know what hope is—what the will to survive is—through their mom. The lessons she's teaching them right now are not lessons you can read about . . . You've gotta live through them."

My Dreams Have Already Come True

Becky reflected on one of her love letters from Tony.

> I think from the moment I met him, something
> I always dreamed about was what our family
> would look like someday. It's something we
> talked about all the time. How many kids do

we want to have? What will our lives look like when we're older? When we were teenagers, he talked about his future: his wife someday, his family someday. But he has grown into such an amazing, incredible human being.

She also spoke about their children. "Mia is brave. She doesn't know it yet. She reminds me a lot of myself when I was little. Mateo is my little warrior."

Tony added, "He's not afraid of anything, you know, but Mateo loves, loves his mom."

"We don't know what's going to happen with me, with my health," Becky said. "But, either way, I think that all my dreams have already come true with them."

She described her ideal legacy. "Any kind of legacy I would like to leave behind is just to love. To love my family, to love God, and to follow him with all your heart."

Becky's Backyard

Since moving into their home, Becky had envisioned enhancements for their backyard. Before she passed away, Tony wanted to build a deck, put up a pergola, and lay sod and paving stones. "Even if for one moment, I can wheel her out there . . . Man, I just gotta get it done."

Heidi LaFleur, the principal at Mia and Mateo's school, launched a GoFundMe. The money would be used for materials, but volunteers would do the work. Their goal was ten thousand dollars. Donors topped thirteen thousand.

In early August, Becky's home bustled. Friends were visiting, bringing food, and checking out the Pedrozas' new backyard. The deck was almost finished. City Hall had provided brick for the patio. Brian Galati, a friend of Becky's sister Alicia, had built an exquisite pergola out of redwood.

A peek at the bench, garden, and pergola

Tiny candles lit the pergola shelves. Purple flowers peeked out of built-in garden boxes. Recessed lights shone on a laminated picture nailed into the center of the seating area.

Their artist friend, Alex Cruz, had created it with a quote from Hillsong's "Oceans." Light streamed over a dark ocean, the lyrics superimposed in a circle of translucent lavender.

With furniture, a fire pit, and a few other finishing touches, Becky's vision for the backyard would be complete. Even on her deathbed, she was making something beautiful.

Sadly, she couldn't see it. In a near coma, she lay in bed, unable to speak or open her right eye.

Her brother-in-law, John, mixed a slab of wet concrete and brought it to her bedside. With help from Tony and Alicia, he pressed Becky's hand into the mix of sand, gravel, and cement. A sweet, musty smell permeated the room. Tony pressed his hand into the mix, next to his wife's. The stone would adorn the backyard garden, near a wooden bench for Mia and Mateo.

That same day, Becky's health plummeted.

Pepper's Very Good Day

Between 9 and 10 that night, the hospice nurse told Tony that Becky could pass away at any time.

Overhearing the nurse, Mariann went into Becky's room and laid in bed beside her daughter. Before she knew it, the whole family was surrounding Becky and singing worship songs.

On August 3, 2016, at 1:13 a.m., Rebecca Pedroza slipped away. She was only thirty-three.

"A gasp of screams wailed over that room," her mom said. "I still can't wrap my head around it. I knew for sure the Lord was going to heal her. He did: He gave her a brand-new body with no more pain in heaven. I can just see her now, trying to rearrange stuff up there."

Becky's cousin Angela posted on her blog. "It was so beautiful. As we were worshipping in the room, she was ushered off into worshipping angels in the Kingdom."

"Our sweet Becky, my girl, is with Jesus." Tony blew out a breath to control his emotions.

"Mia, Mateo, there is no father in God's green earth that is prouder of his children than I am of you," Tony told them. "And if you think I'm this proud, Mommy is so much prouder. I'm actually excited about our future 'cause I know Jesus has so much in store for us. And now that he's got Mommy next to him . . ." Tony turned away, biting his lip.

"We're gonna do great things, kids. We're going to do amazing things in the name of your mother, the best, most amazing woman that ever came into our lives. We got this, kiddos."

At times, her friends and family miss her desperately. But Pepper is having a very good day. This one will last forever.

Chapter Three

Finding God in a Postpartum Fire

Kristina Cowan

T he birth of our babies should be magical. Moms ought to bolt back to life as usual after the most physically challenging experience of our lives. Right? If we believe messages fired at us—on TV, on social media, in personal conversations—we try to live up to the ideal that says, "First comes baby, then comes maternal bliss."

But what if that bliss feels more like a blight?

My first encounter with childbirth blasted me into a veritable fire. The pregnancy was uncomplicated, but childbirth was harrowing. At my OB-GYN's suggestion, I agreed to induce my son's birth ahead of his due date. Scheduling Noah's arrival offered a measure of control. I saw it as a safe way into the otherwise scary world of motherhood. Because the pregnancy had been uneventful, my doctor said it should be simple.

It wasn't.

Heavy doses of labor-inducing drugs jolted my body. In a blink, mild contractions escalated into searing pain. An epidural—something I hoped to avoid—was my last resort. It not only killed the pain, but all my sensation from the waist down. When it was time to push, I couldn't feel my way into doing it well.

I was like a bug flying blind into a zapper.

After pushing for three hours, I was close to fainting, and the baby's heart rate sank. My doctor and I agreed to try forceps. They worked. They also gashed Noah's face and punctured me with a third-degree tear. No one warned me that the tear could lead to complications.

When Noah was two days old, my body shut down. In the middle of the night, I darted into a Chicago emergency room. A double helix of pain and fear choked me. My doctor had stitched my tear so securely, I couldn't go to the bathroom. My body swelled like an overstuffed balloon.

I decided to nurse exclusively, but I hadn't learned to pump. Noah was with me in the ER, asleep in his stroller. What if he stirred while I was with the doctor? Thoughts of him starving rattled my sleep-deprived brain. What if I died from my injuries?

Thanks to the ER caregivers and my OB, my body was soon on the mend. But my mind shriveled. Dark, intrusive thoughts chased me through days dampened by unstoppable crying spells. Brief bouts of sleep were my only reprieve. I was a bad mom for inducing, and I had failed at childbirth. Noah was born in perfect health—minus the forceps' lacerations—but it was despite my shortcomings.

Back then, I didn't know birth trauma put me at risk for developing a postpartum mood disorder. The risk was elevated by the absence of my mom, who died from breast cancer twenty years earlier. Together, they fueled my postpartum depression and hurled me into a furnace with twin blazes—intrusive thoughts and self-condemnation.

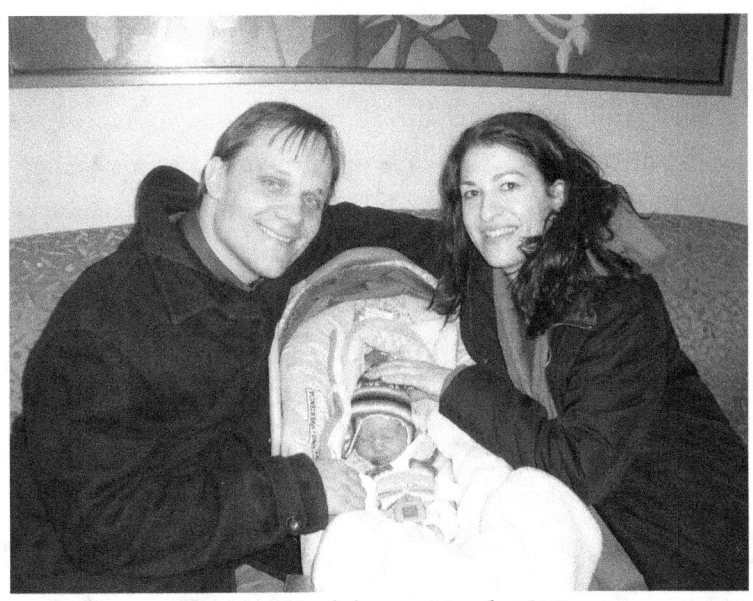

Taking Noah home, March 2009

God With Us

Obsessions, also called intrusive thoughts, and compulsions are the dominant symptoms of postpartum obsessive-compulsive disorder. Intrusive thoughts are persistent, repetitive, and unwanted. They're usually focused on the baby getting hurt, accidentally or intentionally. With compulsions, a mother repeats actions to reduce her fears and obsessions.

I was repulsed by my intrusive thoughts, but they kept coming. Experts remind us that moms—and sometimes, dads—recognize the intrusions as irrational, and they're unlikely to act on them.

One intrusion was fixed on Noah plummeting down the trash chute in our high-rise apartment building. Others centered on forks and frying pans flying into his head.

Danger seemed to be everywhere, even as I walked with the baby down a street or a stairwell. Would I slip? Would a car skid into us? Locked in an endless what-if loop, I cried. Because the images wouldn't stop. Because my mom was gone. Because everyone was kind to me. Because I felt like a failure. My once-peaceful life had burst into flames, and I couldn't see a way out.

In hindsight, I consider the Bible story of Shadrach, Meshach, and Abednego. They too faced a fire, courtesy of King Nebuchadnezzar.

> He ordered the furnace heated seven times
> hotter than usual and commanded some of
> the strongest soldiers in his army to tie up
> Shadrach, Meshach and Abednego and throw
> them into the blazing furnace. So these men,
> wearing their robes, trousers, turbans and
> other clothes, were bound and thrown into the
> blazing furnace. (Dan. 3:19-21)

Such was their lot after refusing to serve the king's gods
and worship his image of gold. Still, they believed the Lord
would deliver them from Nebuchadnezzar's wrath and the
furnace. They gambled big on their faith.

Though the flames killed the soldiers who pitched them
into the furnace, the three men went unscathed—to the
king's great surprise. "He said, 'Look! I see four men walking
around in the fire, unbound and unharmed, and the fourth
looks like a son of the gods'" (Dan. 3:25). Their big gamble
was dwarfed by the Lord, who met them in the furnace and
saved their lives.

Seeing Through the Fire

Shadrach, Meshach, and Abednego trusted God, even in
a fiery pit. I'm not sure I would have been as brave.
My postpartum flames were figurative. But when Noah

was a few weeks old, I too trusted the Lord—no matter what—when I sought help. It was a leap, because we live in an age when stigma and shame shadow mental health.

I didn't hide my tears. I shared my intrusive thoughts with my husband and those closest to me. I called my OB, who recommended antidepressants and talk therapy. I pursued both lines of treatment and found I had postpartum depression. Though I did not have postpartum OCD, I did battle intrusive images, one of its defining symptoms.

Despite my struggles, I didn't despair. Why? Because of God. From the many meals sent by friends and family, to my doctor's compassionate care, to the willingness of others to listen as I retold the story of my traumatic birth—I was cared for. The Lord met me in my furnace.

Through my postpartum fire, I saw Christ more clearly than ever. I felt his dedication to me. I learned to trust him. Time and treatment stitched my frayed ends. By the time Noah was eighteen months old, I was well.

Postpartum depression was a pause button on the fast-forward mode of my everyday life. I learned to savor moments—for a little while, anyway. With my children now wading through the swift K-12 years, I miss that slower pace.

A Unique Loss

Author Jerry Sittser lost his wife, his daughter, and his mother in a car crash. He chronicles the triple-tragedy in his book, *A Grace Disguised: How the Soul Grows Through Loss*. He grieved, coped, and made sense of the losses as they reshaped his soul.

> The accident remains now, as it always has been, a horrible experience that did great damage to us and to so many others. It was and will remain a very bad chapter. But the whole of my life is becoming what appears to be a very good book.[1]

Postpartum depression steals things: Hopes and dreams. Self-worth. Time.

We look back, wishing we could recapture those hours of our discontent. We grieve for what we lost—in the moment, and often, for years to come.

Loss and grief are sure bets in life. The best way to deal with them is not to try to beat them, but to have them join you. With time and practice, we can weave loss and grief into the fabric of who we are. The result is stronger character and unshakable hope. If we can get through grief and loss, we can get through anything.

To borrow Sittser's analogy, postpartum mood disorders are bad chapters. And yet, bad doesn't mean worthless. The most difficult experiences are often the most valuable. We learn and grow more in the shade than we do in the sun. I don't know why, but we do. Sittser points out that his darkest days have made him more aware of God's grace and his need for it.

Although we would rather avoid trials, they're invaluable. They are the "grace disguised" that Sittser alludes to in his book title. Struggles push us to the edge of where we'd like to be—usually, beyond. There, past our edge, is where we can do our best, most life-changing work.

Sittser writes, "It is not, therefore, the experience of loss that becomes the defining moment of our lives, for that is as inevitable as death, which is the last loss awaiting us all. It is how we respond to loss that matters. The response will largely determine the quality, the direction, and the impact of our lives."[2]

For as long as women give birth, mental-health struggles will loom. Instead of worrying about them, we have more powerful alternatives, like praying and talking to others.

Talk about your mental health with other moms, with friends, with professionals. When you share your struggles, others will reach out and help shoulder some of the load. Here, in the rarefied air of sharing the truth, we find lasting comfort and healing.

A version of this essay originally appeared on the Risen Motherhood blog on January 18, 2018.[3]

With Noah in 2015

Author's Note

Part of my response to postpartum depression was to repurpose the struggle into something that would help others. That repurposing became my first book, *When Postpartum Packs a Punch: Fighting Back and Finding Joy.*[4]

It's rooted in the idea that shared stories are healing agents. The book includes my postpartum story, but the focus is on the experiences of other parents across the

United States and in the United Kingdom. It shows and tells what they endured, what their treatment was like, and how they recovered. Theirs is a spirit of overcoming and ultimately, hope—the lifeblood we all need.

Part Two: Memories

"There are better things ahead than any we leave behind."

—C. S. Lewis
The Collected Letters of C.S. Lewis, Volume 3

Chapter Four

Daddy Will and His Million-Dollar Donkey

Christy Brunke

A re you familiar with Mr. Ed, the talking horse? How about Willie, the million-dollar donkey? You may have spotted his T-shirt on FBI agents, or in such faraway places as the People's Republic of China.

But I'm getting ahead of myself. First, I need to introduce my grandfather. One of the most hardworking men I've met, he was incredible with a hammer. Being patriotic, he often wore red, white, and blue. And, though generally quiet, he loved to joke and tell tall tales.

Most people called him Will Reincke. They knew him as a construction manager who supervised prominent building projects like Memorial Stadium, Laurel Park racetrack, and Harrison's Pier 5 in Baltimore's Inner Harbor.

My grandmother called him Will or, sometimes, William. She knew him as the handsome husband she eloped with who provided well for their family. Though Mom-Mom shook her head at his cock-and-bull stories, she loved him loyally until death did them part.

His daughters—Darlene, Debby, and Denise—called him Dad. They knew him as the father who adored them and called them his "Darling D's."

The ten of us grandkids called him Daddy Will. As the oldest, I had the honor of bestowing that nickname. We knew him as the grandfather who loved us, believed in us, and would do anything for us.

In fact, Daddy Will relished spending holidays and vacations with us. Every summer, we spent a boisterous week together in Ocean City. Every winter, we enjoyed quieter weekends—if you exclude the rumble of snowmobiles—at Deep Creek Lake.

When we dined out with him, he always encouraged us to order the most expensive entrées. He wasn't showing off. He just wanted us to have the best life could offer. When we were out shopping, I could never let my eyes rest too long on one object, lest he offer to buy it for me.

One day, when I was a little girl, he set aside his usual courtesy and made one of his customers wait for fifteen minutes. Why? He wanted to finish the page we were coloring together.

Another day, when I was a young woman, he said, "Christy Girl, the man who marries you is going to have to give me a million dollars."

I laughed. "And what would you do with the million dollars?"

"I would give it back to you."

In short, Daddy Will flourished in his construction work, but he saw us as his true treasures. Likewise, he was one of ours.

With six grandkids and a great-niece in Ocean City

Prince of Daddy Will's Petting Zoo

One summer day, Daddy Will brought us to the Maryland State Fair in Timonium. As he admired a white miniature donkey, he told his Darling D's, "I've always wanted a donkey."

They encouraged him to adopt the spotted foal. When they discovered it shared a birthday with Daddy Will, they knew it was fate and named him "Willie."

Given Willie's young age, Daddy Will asked the owner if they could keep his mom for a short time. The owner agreed.

Daddy Will built Willie a shed, but this wasn't your standard donkey lean-to. "Small" wasn't in Daddy Will's vocabulary. When Aunt Darlene requested a shed, he threw up a two-story garage and playhouse. When Mom-Mom asked for a rancher, he included a room big enough to host small wedding receptions. Why should Willie's shed be any different?

For the windows, Daddy Will used Anderson bullet-proof glass from a bank. He installed indoor plumbing and added a ceiling fan for cool shelter on sweltering summer days. Thanks to Daddy Will including a TV in Willie's shed, they could watch *Mr. Ed*, a 1960s sitcom that starred a talking horse.

But the gems of his construction genius weren't the only jewels in Prince Willie's crown. Every day, Daddy Will gave

Willie a peppermint. When it snowed, Daddy Will and my aunts shoveled Willie's pen first, so he and his mom could get around.

When it was time to return his mom to her owner, Daddy Will inspected her accommodations. After all, she too deserved a comfortable place to stay. He learned she would be relegated to a lean-to, so he adopted her and named her "Duffy," after his mother-in-law.

Later, he adopted two miniature goats: a black one, named Billy, and a white one, named Annie. Both relished jumping on Duffy's back and playing on the kids' swing set. But Willie remained the apple of Daddy Will's eye.

Willie, the Million-Dollar Donkey

Willie liked to pluck from Daddy Will's head a hat he often wore. He even chomped a chunk out of the seat of Daddy Will's immaculate, prized truck. My grandfather just laughed.

At one point, Daddy Will commissioned a T-shirt company to design what we now call "The Willie Shirt." The donkey's picture was superimposed on a beach scene, "Willie" scrawled across the top in giant letters. At the bottom, the shirt said, "Ocean City, MD." And the kicker? Daddy Will's estimate of Willie's worth was front and center: $1,000,000.

When Willie turned one, Daddy Will threw him a birthday party. We grandkids wore our Willie shirts. Instead of a candle in the cake, Aunt Debby used a carrot.

Daddy Will ordered Willie shirts in every size imaginable. He kept a big box in their pantry, for friends and family. Like loaves and fishes, no matter how many shirts went out, the box never emptied.

Daddy Will dons his Willie shirt on Willie's first birthday

Mom-Mom didn't know it, but Daddy Will stored a secret stash at Aunt Darlene's house. Whenever the pantry stock dwindled, he added more shirts from her house. It took a long time to deplete the stock. After all, he had ordered three hundred Willie shirts.

My brothers and cousins shared them with friends. Aunt Debby, who worked for the FBI, doled them out to fellow special agents. When I moved to China to teach English at a university, I gave shirts to my teammates. That's how Willie the donkey's fame stretched across the globe.

But life with Daddy Will hadn't always mirrored a Norman Rockwell painting.

Turbulent Times

As a young man, Daddy Will served in Army intelligence during the Korean War. On one dangerous mission, he lost most of his men. Many had wives. Some had children. He had neither. Riddled with guilt, he wondered why he survived while the men with families died.

Of course, this was thirty years before the term "post-traumatic stress disorder" appeared. Instead of pursuing counseling, Daddy Will sought solace in beer and whiskey. For years, he battled alcoholism. Though he was never abusive, his addiction disrupted his wife and daughters' lives.

I was a child at a party in their basement—surrounded by blue-and-red polka dot wallpaper—when someone called an ambulance. Daddy Will had passed out after drinking too much. As the paramedics loaded him onto a stetcher, I wondered whether he would survive.

My mom warned Daddy Will that if he didn't stop drinking so much, she wouldn't let him see her children. By the time my brothers and cousins were old enough to remember, the ambulance calls had ended.

Matters of the Heart

Shortly before I moved to Asia, Daddy Will suffered an abdominal aortic aneurysm. He was only sixty-eight, but we feared the worst.

While he was in the hospital, we prayed often for his health and for his salvation. Did he know the Lord? Would he spend eternity with our Savior? How much longer did we have with him?

Aunt Darlene shared a message with him she had heard while serving at a teen camp. The preacher asked everyone to write down what Jesus would say when they arrived at the pearly gates. Most wrote negative things. The preacher recounted the parable of the prodigal son. Jesus—arms outstretched—would love and forgive them.

After hearing Aunt Darlene's story about the prodigal son, Daddy Will shook his head. "You don't know all the horrible things I've done in my life."

"I know a lot, and it doesn't matter," she said. "If you were going to drown in water—it doesn't matter if you were one-sixteenth of an inch from the surface or a hundred yards—you would still die. God does not measure sin."

Daddy Will was eventually released from the hospital, but we saw no spiritual fruit. Yet, unbeknownst to us, Jesus was calling him. Daddy Will didn't reveal this until the end of his life, but during that season, he often heard Jesus singing to him. He had never heard the song in his life, but it echoed Jesus's words in the Gospel of Matthew.

"Come to me," Jesus sang to Daddy Will, "all ye who are weary and heavy-laden."

Two Letters From China

After I graduated from college in 1999, I moved to Asia. The first summer, I lived in a high rise in Hong Kong.

Every weekday, I clambered onto a crowded subway train that jetted me to an office where I worked as an administrative assistant. On the way home, I studied Mandarin.

While I was in Hong Kong, Daddy Will was diagnosed with cancer. We later learned that, as he battled the disease, Jesus sang to him again, calling Daddy Will to himself.

I sent my grandfather a birthday card with a long message. Woven into my words of love and concern, I shared the gospel.

Before school started that fall, I moved to mainland China to teach. Between the classroom, ministry, and spending time with my students outside of school, my days were full.

In the course of time, Willie fell ill, too. He had developed a hoof disease from eating too many oats.

Daddy Will arranged care for him at a racehorse hospital in Virginia. Aunt Darlene drove the pickup truck while Daddy Will tended to Willie in the trailer.

Even so, the best care couldn't save Daddy Will's beloved pet. Two days after he arrived at the hospital, the doctors put him down, and Daddy Will had him cremated.

Willie's death seemed like a harbinger of my grandfather's passing. I felt compelled to do more than share the gospel in a birthday card. I couldn't live with myself if I didn't do everything I could to ensure his salvation.

Using a pen and several pages of loose-leaf paper, I poured out my heart to him. This time, I didn't hold back. I told him believing in God isn't enough. Even the demons believe and shudder. True faith means a personal relationship with the living Lord. Anything less would result in eternal separation from our Savior. For years, I told him, my greatest fear had been that he would die without being saved.

A Prayer Answered, at Last

After he received my letter, he told Aunt Darlene I was preaching at him. Still, when Pastor Casey met with Daddy Will in the hospital, he understood the gospel. More important, he accepted Jesus Christ as his personal Lord and Savior.

"Will, do you know where you are going?" Pastor Casey asked Daddy Will afterward.

"Yes," he said. "To heaven, where I'm going to build a big house for Betty and the girls and their families to live in."

Mom-Mom and Daddy Will's family in 1988

Pastor Casey later explained to my aunts and mom that he had no doubt Daddy Will was going to heaven.

When I heard he was dying, I flew home. As I slipped into Daddy Will's bedroom, I hadn't yet heard Pastor Casey's story.

Daddy Will was lying on his bed. His weak voice whispered, "Remember what you wrote in your letter?"

I told him I did.

"Let's do that."

I led him in a prayer, asking for God's forgiveness and welcoming Christ into his life.

Soon, Daddy Will—the man who meant so much to all of us—was gone.

Until We Meet Again

Nowadays, when the great-grandchildren gather, my mom sometimes looks at me with a sad smile. "Daddy Will would've loved this."

And he would have.

Though they've never met, a part of Daddy Will appears in each precious child. Michaela's knack for engineering and Jaxon's magnetic tile masterpieces remind me of Daddy Will's gift for building. I catch glimpses of him in Will's charisma, Callum's infectious laughter, Jameson's leadership skills, and Wyatt's sense of humor.

Daddy Will emerges in the mischievous glint in Cameron's eyes. Sometimes he pops up in Fletcher's charm, Trent's boldness, Landon's kindness, or Angelina's playfulness. Noah has his independence. Nolan inherited his love for family.

Daddy Will won't meet his great-grandchildren in this life. He—and they—are missing much.

Still, I eagerly await the heavenly introductions.

For now, we anticipate eternity, that perfect beyond of knowing and being known, loving and being loved.

Chapter Five

Praying Hands: When Art and Faith Collide

Kristina Cowan

I stood in the middle of the Louvre, startled to silence by a piece of art. It wasn't the *Mona Lisa*, *Winged Victory*, or *Marriage at Cana*. It was a postcard print of Albrecht Dürer's drawing, *Praying Hands*, in the museum shop.

Shadowy, rugged, and strong, the hands float in a gray wash on blue paper. My mom, who died of breast cancer almost a decade before, sported a *Praying Hands* lapel-pin as far back as my memory stretched. Her gravestone is etched with a replica of the hands. I didn't know they were Dürer's work until I went to Europe in the late 1990s.

I bought the print and stashed it in my postcard collection. Stowed away in a small box, it laid there for the next fifteen years.

The summer my brother, Jim, sank into a suicidal sea, I remembered the *Praying Hands*. I decked them in a dark-wood frame and gave them to Jim during our last weekend together. My sister and I had flown to see him, and he promised he would make no more attempts on his life. There had been at least ten.

Later that week, he sent me a picture of the print standing on his desk.

"It reminds me to pray," he said. "Thank you."

Those dark days were some of our closest as siblings and friends. My sister and I believed his will to live would help him untangle from the snares of depression. As summer wore on, he appeared to make good progress.

But within a month of our weekend visit, he was gone.

Prayer's Mysterious Power

Jim was just forty-seven when we lost him.

As time passed, I thought about the *Praying Hands*, but I didn't seek to reclaim them. To my surprise, they found me anyway. They hang now in my home, hugged by their careworn frame.

My mom died when she was forty-six and I was fifteen. Back then, I thought she was old. Now that I'm older than she lived to be, I know she was young.

I prayed for her to be spared. Though she wasn't, I continued to pray. I don't know why. Faith is equal parts mystery, diligence, and discovery.

When people leave this earth in the prime of their lives, as my mom and my brother did, it complicates the grieving process. How did my prayers on their behalf enter the mix?

The Christian scriptures' references to prayer, like one in Revelation, bring comfort. Author Philip Yancey explains it well:

> In a scene recorded in the book of Revelation the apostle John foresees a direct linkage between the visible and the invisible worlds. At a climactic moment in history, heaven is quiet. Seven angels stand with seven trumpets, waiting, for about the space of half an hour. Silence reigns, as if all heaven is listening on tiptoe. And then an angel collects the prayers of God's people on earth—all the accumulated prayers of outrage, praise, lament, abandonment, despair, petition—mixes them with incense, and presents them before the throne of God. The silence finally breaks when the fragrant prayers are hurled down to earth: 'and there came peals of thunder, rumblings, flashes of lightning and an earthquake.' 'The message is clear,' comments Walter Wink about

that scene, 'history belongs to the intercessors, who believe the future into being.' The pray-ers are essential agents in the final victory over evil, suffering, and death.[1]

Unexpected Answers

I believe God considers every care we send him. But his methods sometimes disrupt the rhythms of our lives. They are opaque—frightening, even—much as total solar eclipses once were for ancient cultures. Bumbling blind through a blackout, we long for the sun to come pouring out of the sky, to light life's way.

Yet God is not time-bound. To him, our lives are books he knows by heart. He sees how everything will work out.

We are kept by time and its limits, understanding our stories only once we've lived them. Some chapters are unpredictable and scary.

If we had a chance to gaze through a window overlooking the future, we might shudder at the sights. We would try to avoid the bends in our happy roads. But the best stories boast tension-building twists and unusual turns. Those stories develop character.

God is after sculpting us into people of steadfast character. He created us in his image. Bearing his likeness brings pain.

It forces us to get comfortable with the uncomfortable. At times, faith in Christ feels dangerous.

Believing through it all, despite it all, because of it all—that's hard. Unbelief is easier.

When I reflect on losing half of my original family too soon, I can sink into self-pity. All the grief and loss seem unfair.

I was powerless as I watched my mom decline, in part because I was a child. Even as an adult, when I tried to help Jim, I couldn't prevent him from ending his life. Where is God in all of this?

A few times, I've snagged glimpses of him. My encounters with the *Praying Hands* were one of those rare sightings.

Dürer's original drawing resides in The Albertina Museum in Vienna. It was not on exhibit at the Louvre in the late 1990s, when I was there. Museums don't often sell prints of art unless the original is on display in a gallery. The chance I would land on it that day in the Louvre's museum shop was remote.

That it returned to me was unlikely, too.

For me, these are the whisperings of Christ. Subtle cues that he is around, even when the tragic comes to stay. Especially then.

Following Christ does not guarantee freedom from loss, pain, or adversity. What is guaranteed is his presence, through the constancy of the Holy Spirit.

Tragedy has the power to drive us toward despair or deeper into our faith. Our hearts harden. We become bitter. Or we grow from our blows, discovering how they fit into God's purpose for our lives.

The twin tragedies of losing my mother and my brother have changed me. Every day, I wish they were still here. But I have drawn strength from their lives and from their deaths. I see their short existences as animated exclamations, dancing across the page and affirming what's important.

My mom chased her faith and followed Christ at any cost. My brother was faithful to his family and friends, even at his lowest. They both set remarkable examples of living out their faith and loving with abandon. These impressions have left indelible marks on me, like the strong, deep grooves of a canyon.

Strength: I didn't pray for it, but I have received it. It is one of God's answers to my prayers—even if it wasn't the answer I expected.

Covenant Hands

Dürer's *Praying Hands* are one of the world's most well-known pieces of art. Whose hands are they?

Art historians might say they belong to the artist himself, resembling the hands in Dürer's self-portraits.[2] They might point out that the hands were a study for an apostle in an altarpiece,[3] or that Dürer meant them to showcase his talents to clients.[4]

Whatever its earthly origins, the drawing, like any master work of art, beckons us to contemplate something bigger. Part human, part divine, the hands are a mysterious bridge from this world into the next, like the act of prayer itself.

In their humanity, they remind us of Christ, our suffering soulmate. We pray to be spared pain, as Jesus did in Matthew 26:39: "My Father, if it is possible, may this cup be taken from me. Yet not as I will, but as you will." I doubt Jesus prayed expecting he would be spared. He prayed anyway.

In their divinity, the hands remind us of our Savior, who defeated death. His is the original—and only—supernatural power.

The *Praying Hands,* in all their simplicity, symbolize the redemptive arc of Christ's life, death, and resurrection—an arc long and wide enough to reach anyone who dares to believe in it. If we do, we become adoptees into the realm of the Messiah's superpower.

Dürer's hands extend an opportunity to rise with our struggles in tow, and grab hold of the redemptive arc. When we do, we join the arc's eternal story. Within that story, we find strength to overcome our trials and anchor the roots of our belief, no matter the landscape of our lives.

Albrecht Dürer's Praying Hands; The Albertina Museum, Vienna

If you're struggling with suicidal thoughts, please ask for help. If you can't share them with close friends, family, or a therapist, call the National Suicide Prevention Lifeline at 1-800-273-8255.

Chapter Six

Loving People to Their Full Potential

Christy Brunke

I was in my second year serving in the East, starving for a taste of home, when Connie Gibson moved to Nanchang. She brought me warm hugs, contagious laughter, and homemade chicken noodle soup.

Connie wasn't like many fresh-out-of-college recruits from the English Language Institute (ELI). When she landed in Asia, Connie was a fifty-three-year-old grandmother who had just given up a successful career and a stunning California home. She had brokered mortgage loans and taught real-estate finance in the States.

Known as Mom Two, she had opened her home every Sunday for more than a decade to anyone who wanted a meal or a family. "There were only two rules," Connie said, "a hug coming in and a hug going out."

Answering the Call

In February 2000, one of Connie's heart-adopted sons shared with her an ELI ad from *Christianity Today*. It read, "Leave a Legacy—China!" It stirred her long-forgotten childhood dream. She knew God was calling her there. That day, she applied to be an ELI teacher.

Since her own sons were grown and her husband had left her years earlier for another woman, she was free to leave. Her only request? To be in China, but not in a hot region. She couldn't stand the heat.

Six months later, Connie entrusted her clients to a friend and journeyed to Nanchang. Oven-like in the summers, her new hometown was dubbed one of the mainland's Four Furnaces.

Connie accepted this with her usual good-humored wisecracks. Despite the weather, her heavenly Husband had led her to Nanchang. Nanchang was where she would remain.

Becoming Connie Mom

The weather wasn't Connie's only surprise. Chinese nationals rarely hug, even close family members, but Connie saw everyone as a son or a daughter to embrace with God's love. She was soon known as Connie Mom among her students, colleagues, and even the school administrators.

One of her students, Hope, said, "From her, I learned what it is to give, and how warm a hug could be."

Those of us from the States who taught and studied in Jiangxi Province also melted into those hugs. No matter what happened that day or week, we knew Connie Mom would meet us at her door with a bright smile and a big embrace.

Connie at Jiangxi Normal University

Though we often dined in small restaurants, sweat dampening our arms and faces, we spent Sundays at Connie Mom's. In her air-conditioned apartment, we foreigners prayed, worshiped, and shared an American meal. Soup was usually on the menu.

We were mostly young adults, discussing our dreams for the future. What we wanted to become. Where we wanted to go. Whom we wanted to marry.

Her eyes gleaming with delight, Connie counseled and encouraged us. But God hadn't led her east just to impact westerners. She would soon change the face of English-learning in the People's Republic of China.

Coaching Students to Victory

Connie taught English and writing classes, on assignment from Jiangxi Normal University. Of her own accord, she kicked off a translation club, a storytelling group, and speech and public-speaking classes. In her spare time, she founded an English library and held seminars for students and educators across the country.

Two years into her Asia tour, one of her students did what no one from poor Jiangxi had done before. Li Jiayu won second place in a nationally televised English public-speaking competition.

A few years later, Connie's student Ai Lisha won first place in the same competition. By then, it had become the most prestigious English-speaking contest in China.

Connie's motivation was to show people God's love, not to gain recognition. The recognition came anyway. Teachers from top universities who met Connie at contests ended up attending her seminars.

Lina Shi, a teacher at Fudan University, said, "Connie has become a legend in the English public-speaking cause in China. Her passion and dedication have enabled students to rise from obscurity to excellence."

After speaking in Hunan province, Connie signed this student's book, "Wherever you are, be there."

The President to the Proletariat

In 2004, at a state banquet at the Great Hall of the People in Beijing, Connie received a solid gold medallion. She had won the National Friendship Award. The next day, Premier Wen Jiabao congratulated her at a special reception. That evening, she attended a state dinner with President Hu Jintao.

China's largest university press created an award in 2011 just for Connie. In 2014, the China Society for Research on International Professional Personnel Exchange and Development named her the Favorite Foreign Teacher of Chinese Students.

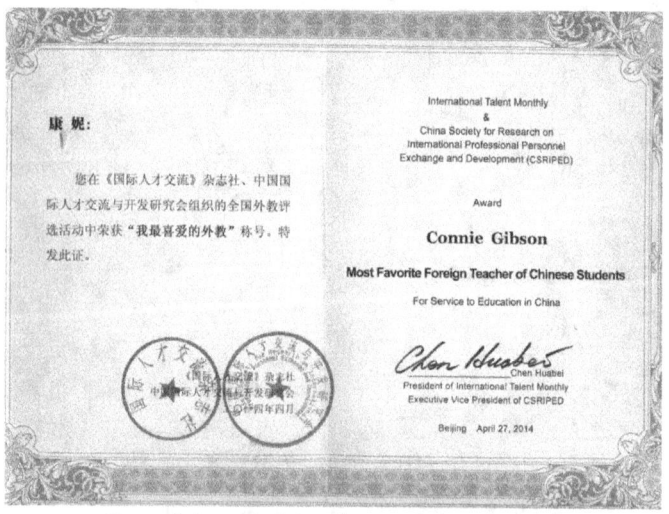

One of Connie Mom's prestigious awards

No matter how famous Connie grew, she made time for ordinary people. She even took her speech class and some visiting Americans to help her clean and paint her favorite hole-in-the-wall restaurant.

"She would hug everyone," said Penny, one of her students. "Flash her huge grin to every passerby, take photos with drivers, gatekeepers, and remember to send them a photo afterwards."

The Secret to Her Success

In 2006, the Foreign Language Teaching and Research Press asked Connie to author a book. They wanted to know how she coached and why her students were successful. Two years later, they published *A Guidebook to English Public Speaking Training*.

What was the secret to her success?

Connie said, "Mostly, I try to see the best my students can be, believe in them and all their possibilities. It all boils down to love. I love them."

Jenny Owens, an American who also taught in Jiangxi Province, saw this love in action. "Many have stared with bug eyes and mouth open because they have never experienced such love," she said. "And those who get a second and third taste usually come back for more. People are seeing Jesus. She has been his hands to so many."

"There is no way I could ever come up with this kind of love myself," Connie was quick to admit. "God has given me this love for them, and for China. Left to my own ability, my passion and love would fall short, dwindle, and die. Only God's continual love and prompting could keep me coming back for fifteen years."

Unstoppable

In December 2010, Connie discovered a lump in her breast. Over winter break, while in the States, she was diagnosed with stage two cancer. By the summer of 2012, it had progressed to stage four.

2012: Connie on China Radio International

Connie knew God wasn't finished with her yet. She had more to do in the East. Despite her illness, she labored on for the good of her students.

Meanwhile, God did his part. When she returned to the States for a checkup in December 2012, she discovered she was in remission.

In December 2014, Connie celebrated her sixty-eight birthday in Nanchang. She taught through the spring 2015 semester before heading back to the West Coast. Though she missed her adopted sons and daughters in Asia, she loved being with her American family, including her two sons and seven grandchildren.

"Even with the cancer, my dear mother has more energy than most people I know," her son Aaron said. "She is, and has always been, an unstoppable force in the field of encouragement for others."

On May 11, five months after Connie celebrated her seventieth birthday, the Lord brought her home. Though we miss her, she's finally at rest and free from pain, relishing her time with her heavenly Husband. I imagine her laughter lighting up heaven, and I look forward to the day she'll embrace me once more.

Her Enduring Legacy

Connie's students have won hundreds of contests and gone on to earn PhDs, land lucrative jobs, and launch successful companies. The effect she's had on our personal and spiritual lives is even more profound.

Eight years after Connie started praying for my future husband, she spoke at our wedding rehearsal. The love she shared continues to inspire me to love people to their full potential.

That love also has inspired TV, radio, and magazine interviews, as well as a short story written by Moira Laidlaw. Connie met Laidlaw in Beijing in 2004, when they both won the National Friendship Award for teaching. After that, they remained in contact by email, becoming close friends.

"I think everyone made exceptions out of Connie," Laidlaw writes, "because she made exceptions out of everyone else. She thought everyone was exceptional."

Maybe that's how we love people to their full potential.

Part Three: Miracles

"If the God who revealed life to us, and whose only desire is to bring us to life, loved us so much that he wanted to experience with us the total absurdity of death, then—yes, then there must be hope; then there must be something more than death; then there must be a promise that is not fulfilled in our short existence in this world; then leaving behind the ones you love, the flowers and the trees, the mountains and the oceans, the beauty of art and music, and all the exuberant gifts of life cannot be just the destruction and cruel end of all things; then indeed we have to wait for the third day."

—Henri Nouwen
A Letter of Consolation

Chapter Seven

Transformed in Ten Minutes: Mom-Mom's Story

Christy Brunke

Indomitable woman though she was, my grandmother had feared death since she was forty. Now, at eighty-five, she was dead. She had flatlined in the hospital, and the nurses struggled to revive her.

Images of Mom-Mom passing before she was ready—before we were ready—shot through my mind.

Mom-Mom was the kind of woman you knew loved you even as she scolded you for lackluster bow-tying skills or an inability to pick decent paint colors. (To her, Betty Jean, the only acceptable hues were bright green or canary yellow.)

She was the kind of woman who always wanted to give you something. You might not know it, but you probably needed a couch from Goodwill, tomatoes from a farmer's market, or peanut butter fudge she'd made with an oar-sized spoon. (Betty Jean made regular trips to The Restaurant Store.)

And she was the kind of woman who always wanted to take you somewhere. Her favorite places were yard sales, Amish country, and the Sight and Sound Theatre. (Betty Jean loved their musicals that bring Bible stories to life.)

Now, she was gone.

Four days earlier, she had been admitted to the hospital for a persistent infection. Her health had been declining on several fronts. Even so, we thought she had at least one more year.

The Day Everything Changed

"Mom-Mom is dying, Christy!" My mother's voicemail turned my blood cold. "She's dying!"

I took a deep breath and called my mom.

After fifteen minutes of CPR, the nurses had revived Mom-Mom. But they didn't think she had long.

Warm tears poured. Mom-Mom was alive. For now.

Driving to the hospital, I faltered between crying out to God, and—submerged in a stunned silence—processing what was happening. I hurried into the ICU, hoping and praying Mom-Mom's heart was still beating.

The waiting room overflowed with family.

*Mom-Mom with her daughters, grandchildren, second husband,
and first four great-grandchildren on her eightieth birthday*

After two hours, we saw her. A ventilator sustained her,
and she couldn't speak, but she knew us and squeezed our
hands.

The next morning, they removed the ventilator, and she
started talking—all about Jesus. She had seen him.

At first, we thought she had met him in a dream. The
more she talked, the more we realized she had glimpsed her
eternal home.

"I know a lot of people there!" She mentioned a door, and
then she described birds, gardens, and a river. "The water is
so beautiful."

"The streets, they are really gold," she told my cousin Abby. "And you should see my house. It's glorious!"

Anyone who knew Mom-Mom knew she was frank, not poetic. In the forty-one years I was blessed to be her granddaughter, I had not heard her use the word "glorious." Now it was a regular part of her vocabulary.

Curious, Aunt Debby asked Mom-Mom, "What does Jesus look like?"

Mom-Mom cocked her head. "It's hard to describe. He's just beautiful."

"What's he doing?" Aunt Debby asked, trying to envision the scene.

"There are many kinds of people in heaven, and he loves and cares for them all. He's always helping people, and I want to go up there and help him."

From Bitter to Blessed

Though some might want to dismiss Mom-Mom's vision as a figment of her imagination, she aced her mental-competency test. What's more, she recognized everyone who visited. Some people she hadn't seen in years. She named all ten great-grandchildren and gave specific instructions for her funeral. Best of all, her relationships with family members were restored.

Over the previous years, a spirit of unforgiveness had taken root in Mom-Mom's heart. This sometimes led to tension in her relationships with her closest family members. Plus, as a woman who had been more than capable, she was frustrated she could no longer do many of the things she loved.

Her daughters were faithful in their visits and care for her, but she was rarely content. As her memory dimmed, she sometimes accused them of lying to or about her. Aunt Darlene, the eldest daughter, often bore the worst of Mom-Mom's ire.

Now clearheaded, Mom-Mom saw her daughters' love for her. She, in turn, lavished them with love and affirmation. "I love you," she said, healing years' worth of heartache. "I love my girls. My girls are wonderful. I have three beautiful daughters."

Aunt Darlene spent that night in Mom-Mom's hospital room. Whenever she moaned or fought her restraints, Aunt Darlene climbed into bed with her and sang hymns into her ear. Two that continue to resonate with Aunt Darlene are "I Love You, Lord," and "The Old Rugged Cross." Soon, Mom-Mom would settle and fall asleep.

How Prayer Postponed Her Passing

As with her daughters, Mom-Mom now showered the Lord with love and affection. She lifted her hands and said, "Praise him! Praise him!"

Mom-Mom told my mother she had always loved Jesus. Regrettably, she wasn't a regular churchgoer. She preferred to stay at home on Sundays, cooking a butter-drenched meal for twenty of us. When she did attend service, she didn't lift her hands in worship. In fact, she called those who did "Holy Rollers." Seeing Jesus had changed everything, even the place she called home.

She had long loved the rancher her husband had built for her, as well as the family that filled it. Now, she longed for the home the Lord had prepared. She grabbed Aunt Darlene's shirt, who marveled at her sheer strength. "You have to let me go," Mom-Mom pleaded. "I want to go. Let me go see Jesus."

"It's okay for you to go to Jesus," Aunt Darlene assured her. "Jesus is waiting."

Mom-Mom beamed and nodded. "Yes." Then she implored the Lord, "Please take me."

Meanwhile, she begged to see her six-foot-three grandson, Ben. If he could break her out of the hospital, she figured, she could return to heaven.

Over the weekend, the hospital staff said Mom-Mom probably had a week or two left. But on Sunday, she kept reaching up for Jesus, saying, "I'm goin' today. Please let me go. Tell the doctors to let me go." Suddenly, she said, "Nope! He postponed it. I'm goin' tomorrow."

We all laughed, but Mom-Mom was right. She didn't pass until Monday, and we were relieved.

Sunday was my cousin Abby's birthday. Her mom and I were praying Mom-Mom wouldn't die that day, but we didn't realize we were praying alike until Mom-Mom was gone. I knew the power of prayer, but seeing a request answered that visibly gave me chills.

Family Here and Beyond

The night before Mom-Mom died, I sat by her bed, giving her sips of ice water.

She called out repeatedly to her mom, as if she could see her. Then she said, "He is so handsome!"

"Who, Mom-Mom? Daddy Will?" I asked, referring to her first husband, my late grandfather.

Aunt Marty thanks Mom-Mom on her seventieth birthday

Mom-Mom nodded and motioned for James Yi, who was sitting in a chair against the wall, to come closer.

A second-generation Korean-American, James attended high school with my youngest brother, Tim. Later, he became Tim's roommate and close friends with my cousins Ben and Sam. Their mom, my Aunt Debby, considers him her third son. Somewhere along the way, we all came to see James as part of the family.

Between wheezing breaths, Mom-Mom croaked, "James . . . is . . . family." The matriarch of our family had declared it, and it would always be so. She charged my mom and Aunt Debby with taking care of him.

Aunt Marty, a niece by birth, cared for Mom-Mom through her final night. Mom-Mom and Daddy Will had raised her from the time she was fourteen. Since then, Marty had been more like a daughter.

The Nurse Manager's Testimony

The next morning, the nurse manager approached my mother. "I heard your mom was speaking," he said with an incredulous stare.

My mother confirmed what he'd heard and told him Mom-Mom had visited heaven.

The nurse manager said she had been clinically dead for at least ten minutes. In fourteen years of nursing, he had never seen anyone come out of that and be conscious—let alone speaking—within days.

My mother opened her Bible to the book of Revelation. She showed him what Mom-Mom had seen: the pure gold streets, the river—bright as crystal—and the people from every tribe, tongue, and nation.

The funny thing was, Mom-Mom wasn't a diligent student of scripture. But everything she described about heaven matched the biblical accounts.

Tears pricked the nurse manager's eyes. "My generation is so weak in faith." He explained that his mom was a strong Christian who had been praying for years for him to return to church. He had three little girls. "I need to get right with the Lord, for them."

Home at Last

Later that morning, another nurse told us Mom-Mom only had hours left.

Friends and family gathered around her at the hospital. We knew where she was headed. We knew she was eager to go. And we knew she was at peace. We were, too.

Soon afterward, Mom-Mom left this life and awoke in the next.

Four days later, I—and others—shared the remarkable story at her funeral. Two hundred people attended. Others live-streamed the event. Still others watched the recording. Many of us have also shared her story in person. How many more will read Mom-Mom's story in this book?

Mom-Mom and Daddy Will built a strong clan that continues to grow and thrive. Unlike many families today, we actually enjoy each other's company. Though we're far from perfect, you could pluck our brood out of reality and place it into a Hallmark movie. This is Mom-Mom and Daddy Will's legacy of love, and it's a rare and marvelous one.

Yet, as much as Mom-Mom lived for her earthly family in this life, one taste of the next, and she was ready to join her heavenly one. Jesus and his family, his legacy, called to her, and she was eager—no, impatient—to heed that call. Her last wish before she died was that each of her family members would know and love her beautiful Jesus.

With Jesus (Steve Abel) at a church musical

During their years together, Mom-Mom and Daddy Will had an open-door policy. Whether you were family, a friend, or a stranger, you were always welcome in their home. Today, they would love to welcome you into their heavenly family and, one day, into their heavenly home.

The door is open. Won't you come in?

Chapter Eight

Somewhere in Time: How Second Chances Heal

Kristina Cowan

F our years ago, my dad died. Twice.

The first time, he was alone, slumped over the wheel of his truck. A swarm of good Samaritans revived him. One smashed through the glass of his passenger door. Several others hoisted him onto the sidewalk. A nursing student skilled in CPR restored his breathing. Emergency workers shocked his heart back to life and sped him to the hospital.

Dad was almost eighty-three, his health declining. His rescuers—a group of average people passing by—managed an uncommon feat. Even an experienced emergency room team would have struggled to do it.

Some of our family believed God had started a miracle in Dad's rescue. Soon he would regain consciousness, and the miracle would be complete. Why else would God have allowed it?

I wasn't so sure. Two weeks earlier, I had talked with my dad about his heart condition. He didn't want procedures to extend his life. "If the Lord wants to take me, it's my time," he had said.

God isn't predictable. I too wondered what he was doing. Dad might die before I reached him. Or he might wake up and go home a changed man. As I tossed my clothes into a suitcase, I braced for whatever awaited on the other side of my plane ride.

With Dad, Easter 2016

A Redemptive Glow

A strong wave of latex and soap hung in the hospital air as my sister, Lisa, and I walked into Dad's critical-care room. We found him cocooned in a web of tubes. Tiny ones wound around his arms and legs, and a ventilator jutted from his mouth. The breathing tube hissed, interrupted by a chorus of chirping monitors. My stomach flattened under an emotional lead balloon.

Occasionally, Dad flailed at the ventilator with a raspy growl, in unconscious slow motion. It was the only time we heard his voice. He never formed words or focused his eyes. They call it life support. But existence support would be more apt.

I had a hunch that he wouldn't return to being the dad I knew.

After a few days, brain tests revealed severe damage. "Seven minutes without oxygen equals brain death," one doctor said. Because Dad had been driving when he lost consciousness, we couldn't be sure how much oxygen he had lost.

We abided by his will and pulled him from life support. Within hours or days, his breath would fade, for good.

Lisa and I prayed for him to go peacefully, with minimal pain. We prayed that we could be with him when he passed.

I doubted the second prayer. I expected a call in the small hours, saying he was gone.

When my mom died, I was fifteen. I held her hand through chemotherapy and radiation. Once doctors could no longer help her, she moved to my grandmother's home in the countryside.

Summer faded, I returned to my dad's house in the city, and I launched my sophomore year of high school. My sister had just given birth to her first child. Neither of us were with Mom the morning she died. My grandmother and uncle stayed with her to the end, and I was grateful she wasn't alone. But I wanted to be there, too.

Whether they failed to call me in an effort to protect me, or if time didn't allow it—I don't know. Still, I felt excluded. My mom was my best friend. The regret I felt for not being with her compounded the loss. Because I was a teenager, my emotional reserve and life experience formed a shallow bed—the perfect place for a thick blanket of guilt.

Mom was irreplaceable. But for thirty years, Dad minded and mended some of the gap. I wanted to be with him when he died.

I sat at his bedside while the tinny pulse of machines pierced and replaced my thoughts. The echoes spun into an odd soundtrack joined by a reel of silent films flashing through my mind.

My parents together in our once-happy home. Our family splintered after their divorce. My mom, in a battle with cancer, dying young. Then marched a parade of images where she was absent, but sorely missed. At last, one I hadn't seen, of them reconciled on the other side of time.

Grasping eternity is a struggle. It often feels distant. That day, it felt like a close companion. A passage into orphanhood—we all dread it—loomed. But I would carry with me a lasting image of my parents reunited. A redemptive glow bloomed over a gloomy week.

Detour to Healing

God seemed to set a miracle in motion by saving my dad's life the first time. Why didn't he finish, and restore him to full health?

For those who lose a parent before adulthood, major life events can spur old grief and longing. I should know by now to expect this. But it still blindsides me.

Woven into my dad's final days was a detour, a new way back to my mom. It allowed me to grieve him and her, as my dual roots. It was a miracle of timing, an oasis for healing from age-old wounds.

The detour stretched out time and tempered the shock that death brings. It would have been tougher to field a call saying he died instantly. That week also let my sister and me experience the loss together.

When my dad died the second time, Lisa and I were with him. A week that had been about dying ultimately held the healing power of life for us both.

Only someone seeing the bigger picture could have orchestrated it. Someone who could intervene and stack up life's ordinary into the remarkable.

Dad proudly served in the U.S. Army in the 1950s.

No Goodbyes

On the day we buried Dad, I woke to the blare of a freight train. I had stayed at my cousin's house for two weeks and hadn't heard a single train. That morning, it sounded like one was chugging through the backyard. The horn sounded at least ten times.

My then-nine-year-old son, Noah, heard it. At the time, and like his papou, Noah adored trains.

When he was born, my dad gave him a relic from his own childhood: a toy train. Made around 1935—the year my dad was born—it was a Hafner O-gauge M10000 Union Pacific streamliner. This so-called toy is now known only to train enthusiasts.

"Mom, that horn was so loud," Noah said. "It went off forever. It had to be Papou."

We buried my dad on a verdant hill overlooking his childhood haunts in Lisbon, Ohio. He had picked the spot a decade earlier. Dad didn't leave anything undone, down to his headstone.

On seeing it etched with a puffing steam engine, Noah's eyes widened. He smiled. "If there are trains in heaven, Papou is driving one."

The human heart isn't wired for separation.

It's unnatural.

Unsettling.

But separation can make us stronger. If we let it, it edges us closer to the golden promise of the Christian faith. A reunion without end awaits us on the other side of forever. It's not just a measure of comfort. It frees us from the weightiness of goodbyes.

As we left the cemetery, I remembered this. "See you later, Dad."

Chapter Nine

When God Walks In: Love's Life-Saving Power

Christy Brunke

W hat if God glided into your operating room and rewrote your life story?

That's what happened to my friend Pete Schoolfield.

Before you raise the red flag of disbelief, know this: Pete is one of the most humble and sincere men I've met. An elder at our church, he exudes compassion, encouragement, and kingdom-purpose. Though he's in his sixties and works full-time as a contractor, his heart for people leads him on mission trips to remote regions of Mexico.

But I'm jumping ahead again. First came the vision.

In 2014, David Platt, a young megachurch pastor, became the president of the International Mission Board. He challenged each church to let God lead them to one of the last six thousand unreached people groups, who have not heard the gospel.

Our senior pastor, Tim Simpson, shared Platt's charge with our church.

It struck Pete like a thunderbolt. God was calling him. The next morning, as Pete prayed and read his Bible, he saw a vision of a lush, green valley.

God spoke to him: "I am going to lead you to this valley. Start praying and gather some people with you to pray for this to happen."

Like Noah with his ark, Pete obeyed.

The Valley From the Vision

Two years later, God led Pete and Pastor Tim, as well as two other men from our church, to central Mexico.

Partnering with a Spanish-speaking missionary, they bumped along perilous roads through mountain passes. At the end of the third, they spotted three crosses in the ground at the edge of a cliff. They stopped, piled out of the Jeep, and inched toward the cliff's edge.

As he peered down into the lush, green valley, Pete's skin tingled.

Pete (right) and Tim (beside him) above the valley

"This is the valley in your vision," Pastor Tim said. "Isn't it?"

Pete turned to him and smiled. "Yes, it is. It is exactly what I saw." Filled with awe and wonder, Pete knew only God could do this. "Thank you," he silently prayed.

After that trip, Pete returned to minister to the Nahuatl people many times. "But do you want to know a crazy thing?" he said. "The next trip to Mexico, when we came to the end of that third pass, those crosses were gone."

Pete and his lovely wife, Diane, embody the love of Christ. Through them and others from our church, the Nahuatl people have experienced Jesus. But their ministry—and Pete's life—soon would be in peril.

The Warning in the Letter

In March 2018, Pete received an alarming letter from his estranged brother. His sister was diagnosed with papillary renal cell carcinoma, a type of kidney cancer that is sometimes hereditary.

Pete, his brother, his sister, and their mother had all endured kidney stones. Since his sister now faced cancer—even though he had no symptoms—Pete pursued testing.

At the hospital, they discovered a malignant tumor in the recesses of his right kidney. Removing it would be formidable, but if they didn't act soon, the cancer would grow.

The surgeon at Pete's practice wasn't skilled in the high-level surgery required for a safe removal. In fact, he said, only three surgeons in the world were. By God's grace, one—Dr. Thomas Jarrett—worked nearby at George Washington University Hospital.

Pete and Diane met with him. "Yeah, no problem," Dr. Jarrett said with a reassuring nod. "I can get it out." They scheduled Pete's surgery for June 14 at Sibley Hospital.

An Albanian Connection

The night before Pete's surgery, their longtime friend Becky Pedneau stayed with them. She would shuttle them to the hospital at 5:30 the next morning.

As Becky would say, she's Diane's "younger friend by ten years and two months." Their friendship began in 1994 when the three teamed up to plan a trip to serve orphans in Albania.

"The bond of friendship that developed through that trip has become one of my dearest blessings," Diane said. "Through Pete's miracle story, I relied on Becky more than any other person, and she never let me down."

God used Becky to weave joy, laughter, and release through the worst days of Pete and Diane's lives. She stood with Diane as the hospital staff wheeled Pete away and remained with her throughout the five-hour procedure. Afterward, they ventured into the recovery room together, neither knowing what to expect.

Molehill, or Mountain?

The surgery was a success. Dr. Jarrett extracted the tumor, two large stones, and a third of Pete's kidney.

The pathology report revealed the tumor was clear cell renal cell carcinoma. Cells from the surrounding tissue tested negative for cancer.

A day after his surgery, Pete was walking and sipping broth and ginger ale. Weaned from the morphine, he was only on Tylenol. He planned to head home in two days.

Then, in the middle of the night, he woke with what appeared to be a back spasm. It turned out to be internal bleeding. Pete's abdomen was swimming with blood.

Pete felt strong the next day—Father's Day—as he welcomed visits from his children and grandchildren. As soon as his oxygen level stabilized, the hospital would send him on his way.

Two days later, he was ready to go home. He wore his "Stanley Cup 2018 Champs" hat emblazoned with the logo of the Washington Capitals. Then his heart rate spiked.

"We have to figure out what's going on," Dr. Jarrett said before ordering scans.

The results showed embolisms lining every chamber in Pete's lungs. An eight-inch clot loomed in his right thigh.

"No way you're going home," the hospital staff said as they rushed him to the Intensive Care Unit (ICU).

Critical Condition

Soon, Pete was bedridden and in critical condition.

Diane peered at the bulb-shaped surgical drain as it topped out with blood and fluid. Five times it filled, faster than it could be emptied. She struggled to stifle a scream. Images of what could happen flashed through her mind. "He's bleeding out!"

"He's not bleeding out," said Dr. Jacob Oppenheimer, Dr. Jarrett's resident. Compassion shone in his eyes. "He's having a bleed." Calmly and professionally, Jacob took charge.

During the next three days, Pete faced still more complications. Finally, Dr. Jarrett said Sibley wasn't equipped for this. In the middle of the night, they transferred Pete to George Washington.

That afternoon, Pete had a three-hour operation to put drains and stents in his legs. They started pumping a blood thinner called heparin. That's when the piercing pain overwhelmed Pete. As a side effect from the surgery, he also became unbearably hot.

Becky and Diane spent all afternoon fanning him from opposite sides of his bed, Becky using her church bulletin.

Nothing worked.

Eventually, the pain overpowered Pete to the point where he didn't even notice the heat. Meanwhile, another scan showed clots engorging his abdomen.

To make matters worse, Diane couldn't stay with Pete overnight at George Washington—as she had at Sibley—so she felt disconnected.

As the jaws of pain clamped down harder, Pete unspooled into incoherence. He continued to decline, inciting the need for an extra—urgent—surgery.

Signing Away Pete's Life

Dr. Sarin, the chief of interventional radiology, pulled Diane aside. "Pete's not able to sign this paper, so I need you to sign it for him. And I need you to look me in the eye and tell me you know he might not come out of it."

After a moment's hesitation, Diane signed the form, her hands trembling. Would Pete survive?

She summoned their son Lucas. Though he had just started a new job, he rushed to her side.

Pastor Tim cried out, "Lord, you can't take Pete! We need him!" He fired off another email to our church's prayer warriors, and then called Diane. She took the call in the hospital lobby, where she was awaiting Lucas.

"Lord, this man is fully committed to you and your Great Commission," Pastor Tim prayed. "He has shared the gospel with unreached peoples in Mexico. We need him healed! And you are the only one who can do this for him."

Clots, Pain, and a New Blood Type?

The surgery was set to take three hours. It took five.

Three hours in, the nurse updated Diane. "We are getting so many clots out of Pete. He's strong, but we're nowhere near done. Dr. Azziz has never seen this many in one person." She cupped her hands. "He has held them in his hands like a pound of hamburger meat. We are still getting clots."

When the surgery was over, Pete continued receiving blood—ten pints total. The average adult body only has eight to twelve. Since Pete was AB negative, the rarest type, they gave him A negative. Pete and Diane wondered: After getting that much blood, did he still have the same blood type?

Back in the ICU, the pain spiked and coursed throughout his body. "And, I mean, I've never experienced pain like that. I really thought I was going to die right then."

They gave Pete oxygen because he couldn't breathe on his own. Weak and wracked with pain, he could barely move.

Doctors and nurses asked, "What's your pain level on a scale of one to ten?"

"I'm way beyond that—I'm up to fifty."

A Last-Ditch Plan

Tuesday night was his worst. "At that point, I realized I was dying. Don't ask me how I knew, but I knew I was dying, and I wasn't going to be able to last much longer."

The doctors hatched a last-ditch plan. Pete had been through so much with the clot surgery, they hadn't reached his legs. The surgical team would determine if Pete's abdomen was clear. Then, they would re-evaluate his legs.

Their daughter-in-law Jolie drove three hours to be with them. She hadn't seen him since Father's Day. "Mom, how long has he looked like this?"

Pete was too weak to push the button for his pain medicine, even when they placed his finger on it. The nurse allowed Diane and Jolie to push it for him.

The last thing Pete wanted to hear before the hospital staff rolled him away was the scriptures. He motioned Jolie closer. Though he could only whisper one word every fifteen seconds, he asked her to read his favorite psalm: Psalm 61.

She did. Then she read Diane's favorite: Psalm 139.

Pete drew Diane near and said, "Diane, I'm dying." He said it once more, this time with finality: "Diane, I'm dying."

"I've never seen him so weak." Diane shook her head. "I didn't think it was possible for this strapping man to be so weak."

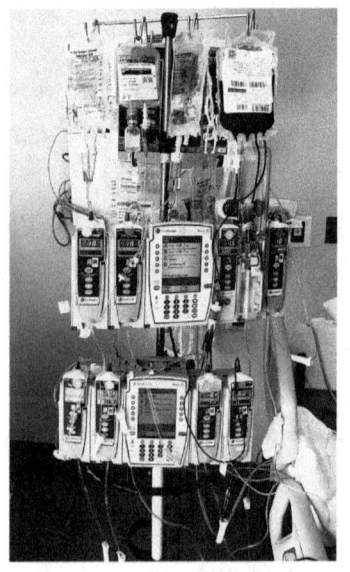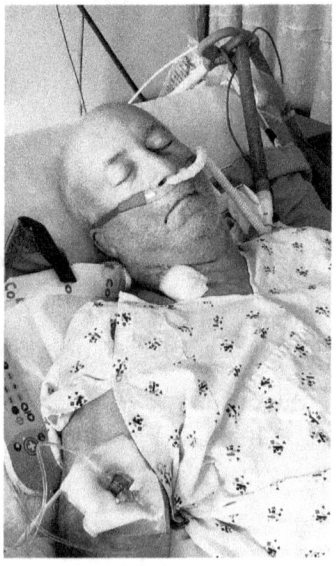

Pete near death with his bags and monitors

The Curveball

The surgery was expected to take several hours, so Diane and Jolie headed to lunch.

Not even an hour passed before Diane's phone rang. It was Dr. Sarin. Her heart throbbed in her throat. Was Pete gone?

"Diane, medically, there was nothing we could do for Pete. The heparin is doing its job. We went back in through his neck, and no new clots had formed."

Pain pierced the back of her throat as Dr. Sarin's words echoed. *There was nothing we could do for Pete.* He was alive, but in the same awful condition.

Diane and Jolie hurried back to the hospital. When Diane saw Pete, she stopped mid-stride and gasped.

He was sitting up, talking.

She stared at him incredulously.

He caught her right hand and feather-kissed it, making her skin tingle. "Your love saved me," he whispered. Then he clutched her left hand and kissed that one too. "Your love saved me."

Diane's breath hitched. What did he mean?

God of All Comfort

When Pete spoke to Diane before the procedure, he wanted her to be ready for his passing. "I accepted Jesus when I was

127

seventeen, and I knew I was going to heaven. And, in dying, I was kinda like, 'This is great! I'm gonna wake up in heaven!' At the same time, I didn't want to leave Diane."

In the operating room, before Pete received the anesthesia, he had the encounter of a lifetime.

> All of a sudden, God came into the room—God himself—and sat next to me. I could feel that he knew how much pain I was in, and his voice flooded my soul with sympathy and compassion. That was the first time I had felt something other than pain for days and days, and it was wonderful.

Pete exhaled. His suffering would finally be over. Even doctors and medication couldn't relieve the relentless pain. Surely, God was here to take him home.

"It's Not Your Time"

God's head wasn't visible to Pete—his face was shrouded—but he wore a gleaming white tunic.

When Pete found his voice, he said, "God, you know I'm about to die."

"Yes, I know," said a voice so clear, deep, and rich, it could only emanate from the King of Kings.

Then Pete remembered something Jesus said on the Cross. "Father, into your hands, I commit my spirit," Pete echoed. "You gave me my spirit when I was born, and now I am giving it back to you. Just take it, and take me home."

God raised his left hand, a hand so big it could easily wrap around Pete's thigh. "No, Pete. It's not your time."

"He just called me by my name!" Pete thought. But he said, "What do you mean it's not my time? Look at me. I'm just about dead. I can't live like this. If you're not going to take me home, what are you going to do?"

"I can't believe I talked to God like that," Pete later said. "But I was almost dead, so I figured, what the heck?"

God put his enormous hands together, and in them appeared a clear ball, like the many points of a star. "I just put some of my love inside this ball." He held the ball in his right hand, reached into the darkness with his left, and came back with a smaller ball. "I just took some love out of Diane." Then he switched hands and put another clear ball into the bigger ball. "I just took some love from your four boys."

"I'll never forget how sweet and gentle he was," Pete told our congregation months afterward. "And he just put it in my mouth. You know those little breath strips, and you put them in your mouth, and they dissolve? It was like that. It dissolved in my mouth, and I felt it go down.

"Then I felt this renewal go down, all the way to my toes. Just like that, all my pain was gone. I mean, I had been in agony for three days, and then he flicked a switch, and it was gone. And then, God was gone."

Soon after, Pete was put under anesthesia, so Dr. Sarin could reduce the clots in his legs. But when Dr. Sarin went in, the clots were disappearing, and no new ones were forming.

Pete was healed.

The surgeons had nothing more to do.

Alive and Reunited

When the hospital staff rolled Pete back to his room, Jolie turned to Diane. "Mom, we are witnessing a miracle."

The tension that had been squeezing Diane's heart for weeks suddenly loosened. Warm tears spilled down her cheeks. Everything would be fine.

The next morning, Pete sat in a chair and ate something solid for the first time in a week: Jell-O. Even better, Diane could finally hug him.

Two days later, Pete moved from the ICU into a telemetry room, where he spent a few more days.

On July 5, Pete finally went home. He had been in two hospitals for twenty-two days. Eleven of those he spent in three ICUs, seven of those bedridden. He had faced five surgeries, two of them five hours long. Throughout the process, he lost forty pounds and received ten pints of blood. "I would be dead if God hadn't come and met me like that."

Teodora and You

Today, Pete and Diane continue to serve in our church, blessing everyone around them.

Pete and Diane on a cruise a year later

In 2019, a year after God walked into his operating room, Pete returned to Mexico. Their team hiked to remote villages in the mountains. At each home, Pete shared his miracle story.

In one, a woman named Teodora asked Jesus into her heart. A year later, Teodora gave birth to a baby girl.

God used Diane's love to save Pete, and Pete's love to save Teodora. Will he use Teodora's love to save her daughter?

Pete sharing his miraculous story with Nahuatl children

For Pete, his experiences confirm what the Bible teaches. "And we know that in all things God works for the good of those who love him, who have been called according to his purpose" (Rom. 8:28).

God's love saved Pete, spiritually in his teens, and physically in his sixties. Pete's greatest desire is that God would save you too. Will you let him?

Epilogue

Kristina Cowan

C.S. Lewis drifted into a soul-wrenching despair after losing his wife and soulmate, Joy. His once-vibrant world was awash in dismal gray. A man of uncommon brilliance, Lewis unraveled with his grief—an experience shared by many of us. In *A Grief Observed*, he writes:

> On the rebound one passes into tears and pathos. Maudlin tears. I almost prefer the moments of agony. These are at least clean and honest. But the bath of self-pity, the wallow, the loathsome sticky-sweet pleasure of indulging it—that disgusts me. And even while I'm doing it, I know it leads me to misrepresent [Joy] herself.[1]

What little time Lewis had with his wife may have complicated his anguish. When he married Joy, she was terminally ill with cancer. She died several years later.

As Madeleine L'Engle points out, "He had been invited to the great feast of marriage and the banquet was rudely snatched away from him before he had done more than sample the hors d'oeuvres."[2]

The loss shook his pillar-like faith. His sense of God abandoning him was profound.

> But go to Him when your need is desperate, when all other help is vain, and what do you find? A door slammed in your face, and a sound of bolting and double bolting on the inside. After that, silence. You may as well turn away. The longer you wait, the more emphatic the silence will become.[3]

It's easier to comprehend the intensity of his despair when we consider the intensity of his love. In the introduction to *A Grief Observed*, one of his stepsons, Douglas Gresham, sheds light on Lewis's unique bond with Joy:

> Much has been written, both fictional and factual (sometimes one masquerading as the other) concerning their lives and their meeting and marriage, but the most important part of

the story pertaining to this book is simply a recognition of the great love that grew between them until it was an almost visible incandescence. They seemed to walk together within a glow of their own making.[4]

Another Christian philosopher who experienced soul-stinging loss was Nicholas Wolterstorff. His adult son perished in a mountain-climbing accident in 1983. In his book, *Lament for a Son*, he raises questions about grief that mirror Lewis's reflections.

How is faith to endure, O God, when you allow all this scraping and tearing on us? You have allowed rivers of blood to flow, mountains of suffering to pile up, sobs to become humanity's song—all without lifting a finger that we could see. You have allowed bonds of love beyond number to be painfully snapped. If you have not abandoned us, explain yourself.[5]

Both men sank into the mire of their grief. They afforded themselves time. They allowed their groans to take shape as words on a page.

Though they sank, they didn't get stuck.

They plodded through the valleys, grimace by grimace. Along the way, the God of the Bible revealed himself, encouraging their downcast hearts.

Free Will's Double Edge

Later in his grieving process, Lewis writes:

> I have gradually been coming to feel that the door is no longer shut and bolted. Was it my own frantic need that slammed it in my face? The time when there is nothing at all in your soul except a cry for help may be just the time when God can't give it: You are like the drowning man who can't be helped because he clutches and grabs. Perhaps your own reiterated cries deafen you to the voice you hoped to hear.[6]

Roadblocks and walls built by our own hands: We excel at getting in our own way, in grief as in the rest of life. Call it myopia, blindness, or turning a deaf ear—the results are the same. We choose not to receive what God gives us. We might do it on purpose, or unwittingly.

We have the choice because God places a high premium on our right to choose. When he created mankind, he wired us with free wills, not a robotic script.

Our free wills bear a double-edge, of course. We might wield them in remarkable, life-giving ways. Or we can brandish them as tools of destruction. If we remember this in our grief—that we might be the biggest hindrance to our own healing—we're a step closer to the bounty God promises.

He is not absent in our grief, nor does he want us to be in permanent despair. Taking it further, if we contemplate what our free wills say about our Creator, we gain a clearer understanding of him.

Os Guinness, a prominent author and social critic, makes a strong case for why God doesn't encroach on the human will. God's respect for human integrity is so great, Guinness says, he limits his own freedom regarding our choices. "The one place God does not invade or override is the human heart and conscience," he writes.[7]

By setting an example of restraint and respect, God calls us to the same behavior, both toward other human beings, and toward him. If we follow his lead, and ultimately accept Christ as our redemptive Savior, it's an authentic choice on our part.

More than anything, I believe God is after an authentic relationship with us. Not giving up on him when we grieve breeds that sort of authenticity. Looking back on seasons of deep grief, we just might see that by clinging to our faith, it grows deeper.

Comfort Amid the Mystery

Mystery is an inescapable part of grief and loss. We crave the reasons behind why we must suffer and lose. As Wolterstorff writes:

> We strain to hear. But instead of hearing an answer we catch sight of God himself scraped and torn. Through our tears we see the tears of God. A new and more disturbing question now arises: Why do you permit yourself to suffer, O God?[8]

Like Lewis, Wolterstorff made discoveries as he moved through his despair. Instead of an explanation for suffering, he found God suffering alongside us. If God explained the mystery of suffering and loss, would it satisfy our human intellect? Maybe. I doubt it would satisfy the human heart.

The God of Abraham, Isaac, and Jacob is unconventional. He takes the road usually avoided. By grieving with us, he relieves some of the burden from our weighed-down hearts. This willingness to join us in the trenches—it's a reminder that he doesn't send us anywhere he himself hasn't navigated.

Ultimately, our faith calls us to be at peace with the reality that faith involves mystery. God doesn't promise that his ways will be clear. Isaiah 55:8 says, "'For my thoughts are not your thoughts, neither are your ways my ways,' declares the Lord."

Sometimes, our rearview mirror illuminates his methods; they make sense. Other times, we gain no such insight. We don't find all the answers in this life—not when we glide along in the sunlight, not when we're deep in darkness. That shouldn't weaken our faith. God is still who he says he is. Hebrews 11:1 says, "Now faith is confidence in what we hope for and assurance about what we do not see."

The Long Arc of Legacies

Life is often a cycle of opposing forces. Like dynamic fiction defined by plots of tension and release, so go the true stories of human existence. Like engaging musical scores, we encounter consonance and dissonance. Like captivating art that employs a technique called chiaroscuro, our lives are as studies of light and darkness. We journey through grief to joy, and back again.

The best art, music, and literature are shaped and strengthened by opposing forces which are, at their core, grief and joy. They likewise shape and strengthen our faith as believers in Christ. Through the friction they bring, we uncover new sides of ourselves and God. The push-and-pull of life draws us deeper into a relationship with him.

G.K. Chesterton said, "I had always felt life first as a story: and if there is a story there is a story-teller."[9]

Mysteries and unanswered questions are essential to keeping readers engaged in a story. We don't question authors when they use these tools. They do it to build character and send a message. Why do we then question God when he allows mysteries and unanswered questions into our lives?

Loss is weaved into the fabric of every human story. For some of us, that weaving begins early, in childhood. For others, it is later in life. No matter the nature or timing of a loss, we are called to overcome the challenges it poses.

In that overcoming, we find something far better than answers or unraveled mysteries. We land on our legacies: the spiritual inheritance we leave for those who come after us. In all their richness, those legacies linger long after our short time on earth.

Notes

"As the rain hides the stars ..." George Appleton, ed., *The Oxford Book of Prayer* (Oxford: Oxford University Press, 1985), 58.

Part One: Mourning

"And there is a similar distinction ..." G. K. Chesterton, "The Character of King Edward," *The Illustrated London News,* June 4, 1910.

Chapter One: My Mother, Myself

[1] Maxine Harris, Ph.D., *The Loss That Is Forever: The Lifelong Impact of the Early Death of a Mother or Father* (New York: The Penguin Group, 1995), 199.

[2] Ryan Howes, "Happy Thanaversary: The Day of Passage," *Psychology Today,* August 30, 2012, https://tinyurl.com/mpjha26u.

[3] Hope Edelman, *Motherless Daughters: The Legacy of Loss* (Reading: Addison-Wesley, 1994), 283.

[4] Aleksandr Solzhenitsyn, "A World Split Apart" (commencement address, Harvard University, Cambridge, MA, June 8, 1978).

[5] Bethany Williamson, "And He Will Purify: Abiding in His Refining Light," *The Advent Project* (devotional), Biola University, December 9, 2020, https://tinyurl.com/yckx5ttt.

[6] Nicholas Wolterstorff, Ph.D., *Lament for a Son* (Grand Rapids: Eerdmans, 1987), 81.

[7] Harris, *The Loss That Is Forever,* 13.

[8] *BookLife,* review of *When Postpartum Packs a Punch: Fighting Back and Finding Joy,* by Kristina Cowan, *Publishers Weekly,* September 18, 2017, https://tinyurl.com/yckr3fxf.

[9] Dean Lane, email message to author, September 19, 2017.

[10] Jennifer Kromberg, "How Dads Shape Daughters' Relationships," *Psychology Today,* July 1, 2013, https://tinyur l.com/dxdrfsud.

[11] Montreal Neurological Institute/McGill University, "The Blind Really Do Hear Better," news release, July 23, 2004, https://tinyurl.com/bdz38mmj.

[12] Edelman, *Motherless Daughters,* 181.

[13] *Merriam-Webster Online,* s.v. "independent," accessed January 21, 2022, https://tinyurl.com/4wbn8nnz.

[14] Harris, *The Loss That Is Forever,* 139.

[15] Ann Voskamp (@annvoskamp), "In tumultuous times, there is only One Voice that can calm seas," Instagram, January 11, 2021, https://tinyurl.com/2p8azh3b.

Chapter Three: Finding God in a Postpartum Fire

[1] Jerry Sittser, *A Grace Disguised: How the Soul Grows Through Loss* (Grand Rapids: Zondervan, 2004), 212.

[2] Sittser, *A Grace Disguised,* 17.

[3] Kristina Cowan, "Finding God in My Postpartum Fire," *Risen Motherhood* (blog), January 18, 2018, https://tinyurl.com/2p8ct58u.

[4] Kristina Cowan, *When Postpartum Packs a Punch: Fighting Back and Finding Joy* (Amarillo: Praeclarus, 2017).

Part Two: Memories

"There are better things …" Walter Hooper, ed., *The Collected Letters of C.S. Lewis, Volume 3: Narnia, Cambridge, and Joy 1950-1963* (San Francisco: HarperSanFrancisco, 2007), 1,430.

Chapter Five: Praying Hands

[1] Philip Yancey, *Prayer: Does It Make Any Difference?* (Grand Rapids: Zondervan, 2006), 130.

[2] Martin Bailey, "Dürer used his famous Praying Hands drawing to advertise his talent," *The Art Newspaper*, December 4, 2018, https://tinyurl.com/38786uzf.

[3] Andrew Robison and Klaus Albrecht Schröder, *Albrecht Dürer: Master Drawings, Watercolors, and Prints from the Albertina* (Washington: National Gallery of Art, 2013), 176.

[4] Bailey, *The Art Newspaper*, https://tinyurl.com/38786uzf.

Part Three: Miracles

"If the God who revealed life to us …": Henri Nouwen, *A Letter of Consolation* (San Francisco: Harper & Row, 1982), 78.

Epilogue

[1] C. S. Lewis, *A Grief Observed* (San Francisco: HarperSanFrancisco, 2001), 4.

[2] Ibid., xii.

[3] Ibid., 6.

[4] Ibid., xxiii-xxiv.

[5] Wolterstorff, *Lament,* 80.

[6] Lewis, *A Grief Observed,* 46.

[7] Os Guinness, *The Magna Carta of Humanity: Sinai's Revolutionary Faith and the Future of Freedom* (Downers Grove: InterVarsity Press, 2021), 55.

[8] Wolterstorff, *Lament,* 80.

[9] G. K. Chesterton, *Orthodoxy* (New York: John Lane, 1908), 110.

Photo Credits

My Mother, Myself
- First photo courtesy of the Lane family.
- Second photo courtesy of the Lane family.
- Third photo courtesy of the Cowan family.

Pepper's Very Bad Day
- First photo courtesy of Rebecca Pedroza.
- Second photo by Natalie Hantosh.
- Third photo courtesy of Stephanie Hubert.
- Fourth photo courtesy of Mariann Rodrigues.
- Fifth photo by Amor in Motion.
- Sixth photo courtesy of Mariann Rodrigues.

Finding God in a Postpartum Fire
- First photo courtesy of the Cowan family.
- Second photo by Elisabeth Oda.

Daddy Will and His Million-Dollar Donkey
- First photo courtesy of Darlene Carter.
- Second photo courtesy of Denise Litzau.
- Third photo courtesy of Christy Brunke.

Praying Hands
- Photo courtesy of The Albertina Museum, Vienna.

Loving People to Their Full Potential
- First photo courtesy of Connie Gibson.
- Second photo courtesy of Connie Gibson.
- Third photo courtesy of Connie Gibson.
- Fourth photo courtesy of Connie Gibson.

Transformed in Ten Minutes
- First photo by Becca Doring Photography.
- Second photo courtesy of Marty Wade.
- Third photo courtesy of Steve Abel.

Somewhere in Time
- First photo courtesy of the Cowan family.
- Second photo courtesy of the Lane family.

When God Walks In
- First photo by Jon Brawley.
- Second photo by Diane Schoolfield.
- Third photo courtesy of Diane Schoolfield.
- Fourth photo courtesy of Pete Schoolfield.
- Fifth photo courtesy of Pete Schoolfield.

Discussion Questions

When *Losses Become Legacies* is ideal for book clubs. With nine stand-alone stories, even if members miss a chapter, it's easy enough to jump back in for the next one. Plus, everyone has faced loss, in one way or another.

Would you like the authors to join one of your meetings by phone, Zoom, or FaceTime? Email us here:

- christy@redemptiveedgepress.com
- kristina@redemptiveedgepress.com

In the subject line, write "Book Club" and include the requested date. Suggesting an alternate date or two would be helpful.

General

1. What comes to mind when you think of the word "loss?"

2. What losses have you faced? Loss of health, a marriage, or a loved one are three big ones mentioned in the introduction. Others include the loss of your house, job, family, or reputation.

3. In the nine stories, what sorts of losses did the authors and main characters encounter?

4. What comes to mind when you think of the word "legacy?"

5. In what ways have others' legacies blessed your life?

6. What kind of legacy do you want to leave?

Introduction

1. Does God relate to our suffering?

2. The Cross symbolizes both suffering and salvation. How has Christ's loss been transformed into legacy, both for him and for us?

3. How is losing your mom when she's young different than losing your mom when she's older? How is it the same?

One: My Mother, Myself

1. Explain the different roles Kristina's dad and mom played in her childhood.

2. What did she learn from each of them?

3. What is a "thanaversary?" What year did Kristina reach hers? How was this significant?

Two: Pepper's Very Bad Day

1. Who or what was Becky's source of peace throughout her battle with cancer?

2. In what ways did she face her losses with joy, strength, and beauty?

3. What is her legacy?

Three: Finding God in a Postpartum Fire

1. How is postpartum depression a loss?

2. Why didn't Kristina despair?

3. How did she repurpose her pain from her perinatal mood disorder into a legacy?

Four: Daddy Will and His Million-Dollar Donkey

1. What made Will Reincke an extra-special grandfather?

2. What important decision did Daddy Will make toward the end of his life? Who or what led him there?

3. When you reflect on your own hard times, where have you seen God working behind the scenes?

4. What can you do to encourage your heart to trust God when you can't see what he's doing?

Five: Praying Hands

1. How does suicide complicate the grieving process?

2. What did the *Praying Hands* symbolize to Kristina, her mother, and her brother?

3. How did the *Praying Hands* reappear providentially throughout Kristina's life?

Six: Loving People to Their Full Potential

1. If Connie's husband hadn't left her years before, do you think she would have moved to China?

2. Romans 8:28 says, "And we know that in all things God works for the good of those who love him, who have been called according to his purpose." How have you seen God use bad circumstances in your life and others' lives for good?

3. What was the source of Connie's lavish love for others? How do you think she was continuously filled, so she was able to pour out in such an extraordinary way?

Seven: Transformed in Ten Minutes

1. How was Mom-Mom's fear of death replaced with a longing for heaven?

2. What other transformations took place after she saw Jesus?

3. Why was the nurse manager so surprised Mom-Mom was speaking? How did this impact his walk with Christ?

Eight: Somewhere in Time

1. Why do you think the Lord allowed Kristina's dad to die twice?
2. What closure and healing happened for Kristina and her sister during those few days?
3. Have you had a similar experience?

Nine: When God Walks In

1. Do you believe God still performs miracles today? Why or why not?
2. How did Diane's love save Pete?
3. Why do you think God might have extended Pete's life?

Epilogue

1. According to Nicholas Wolterstorff, how does God redeem us from suffering?
2. What do we gain—by God's grace—as we overcome the challenges posed by loss?
3. What's the most important thing you're taking away from this book?

Acknowledgments

Christy Brunke

"As iron sharpens iron, so one person sharpens another" (Prov. 27:17).

Kristina, your edits make my writing so much stronger. Your friendship and partnership in prayer mean even more. I couldn't think of a better person to write, edit, and publish a book with. God's hands are all over our friendship and the work we do together.

Matt Cowan, thank you for helping us with the technical aspects of publishing this book. Better still, thank you for opening your home to the Brunke Bunch.

Pepper, as I read through three years of your blogs, you partnered with me in telling your story. Thank you for sharing yourself and your experiences so candidly. I miss you, my friend, and look forward to seeing your signature grin again in heaven.

I also want to thank your friends and family for all their help. I'm particularly indebted to your mom, Mariann Rodrigues, and your sister Stephanie Hubert. Through shared resources and answering my endless questions, they filled in the blanks. Without them, "Pepper's Very Bad Day" wouldn't be as complete, accurate, or beautiful.

Amor in Motion, I'm grateful for the poignant film you created about Becky and Tony. I watched it many times—tissues in hand—while researching Rebecca Pedroza's story.

Abby Braswell, Darlene Carter, Debby Russell, and Denise Litzau, thank you for helping me with the details of Mom-Mom and Daddy Will's stories. Above all, thank you for being vessels of God's love and lifelong sources of blessing.

Connie Mom, I'm tearing up even as I type this. Thank you for being my second mom in China and beyond. Years ago, through shared resources and email interviews, you told me your story. Today, it's finally in print.

Andy Scheer, thank you for applying your editorial expertise to Connie's story during *The Art of Short Nonfiction* course.

Joshua Holec, your vision statement inspired the title of Connie Mom's story. Thank you for being epic.

Michael Gibson, thank you for your encouragement and for supplying more details after your mom passed away.

Pete and Diane, you are one of the sweetest, godliest, most encouraging couples I've met. With every encounter, you lift my spirits and lighten my way. Thank you for telling me your story and allowing me to share it with the world.

Pastor Tim Simpson, I couldn't ask for a better senior pastor for Mark and me to serve under. Thank you for your help with this story and for inspiring our church to reach the nations.

Dad (Mike Litzau) and Uncle Wayne (T. W. Carter), thank you for proofreading our proof copies. Did you cach the typos in this sentince?

My darling husband, Mark, I appreciate your big-picture perspective. Your suggestions helped me cut the boring parts and improve the important ones.

Our daughters, Michaela and Angelina, thank you for sharing Mommy with my book baby.

Most of all, praise and glory go to my Lord and Savior, Jesus Christ. Without him, these stories—and mine—would all have different endings.

Acknowledgments

Kristina Cowan

By the time I read Hope Edelman's groundbreaking book, *Motherless Daughters*, my mom had been dead for five years. Edelman's words brought comfort. "Our lives are shaped as much by those who leave us as they are by those who stay. Loss is our legacy. Insight is our gift. Memory is our guide."

In my twenties, I donned the motherless mantle as at least half of my identity. Motherhood eventually pried me away from that notion. As a parent in my thirties, I began to grasp the meaning of loss as a legacy.

Edelman's words have stayed with me for almost thirty years. They inspired part of the title of this book. I'm grateful she chose to cover a topic many would rather avoid. Her work has paved the way to healing for countless motherless daughters.

I owe Christy Brunke a debt of thanks, for partnering with me to imagine this book into being. Her sharp storytelling skills and editorial acumen have ensured that each piece shines. Her unflagging joy and humor have made this project more fun than work.

Michelle Argyle, your artistic genius helped us achieve our cover goals. Christy and I are grateful for your patience and expert input as we worked through several renditions.

My husband, Matt, works diligently to support our family and my writing life. I couldn't do it without him.

My sister, Lisa, read the early versions of several of my essays, especially "Praying Hands." She is a constant source of encouragement in my work and everyday life. I would be a different person without her influence.

My dad and my brother were my moorings for many years. Like a good education, their influence continues, even in their absence.

I have my mom to thank for my enduring quest for a deeper faith. If she hadn't been a follower of Christ, there's a good chance my curiosity about him wouldn't have surfaced as early as it did.

To my friends Diana, Rita, Julie, Jenn, Lynn, and Kelly—thank you for cheering me on and reading whatever I send you. Writing is a solitary pursuit. Drawing friends into the fold makes it less so.

And to the God of all comfort, thank you for walking with me along life's redemptive edges.

A Note From the Authors

We pray our book ministered to you. If you have a moment, would you write a review on Goodreads, Amazon, or wherever you bought or borrowed it? Even one or two sentences could make a huge difference in helping other readers find this book. For Amazon, you can use this QR code:

Thank you for helping more people turn their losses into legacies!

—Christy & Kristina

Also by Christy Brunke

Also by Kristina Cowan

About the Authors

Christy Brunke

Christy is the bestselling, award-winning author of the novel, *Snow Out of Season*. A mom, pastor's wife, and former missionary, the Lord has led her on adventures here and abroad.

Though she's written hundreds of shorter nonfiction pieces, this is her first book in that realm. She hopes her creative recounting of these true stories will inspire you to worship.

Read a free short story and an excerpt from her novel at ChristyBrunke.com. Download a free eBook and learn about her battle with Lyme disease at OurLymeJourney.com.

Want to connect with Christy on social media? Here's how:

- Facebook.com/ChristyBrunkeAuthorPage
- Instagram: @christybrunke
- Pinterest.com/christybrunke

About the Authors

Kristina Cowan

Kristina was born in Ohio in the middle of the worst fashion decade of the modern era. (You guessed it: the seventies.) Until the space shuttle *Challenger* perished, she hitched her wagon to the stars, hoping to be an astronaut.

Soon after, she landed on her other love, writing. She's been doing it since, covering everything from education to women's issues to 9/11. Her first book—*When Postpartum Packs a Punch*—delves into the issue of new parents' mental health.

She earned graduate and undergraduate degrees from Northwestern University, in journalism and speech. A former full-time journalist based in D.C., she used to chase stories on Capitol Hill and across the country. Now a married mom and freelancer in Chicagoland, she chases stories with more forgiving deadlines—along with her kids, cats, and English cream retriever. Catch up with her at her website, kristinacowan.com, or on Instagram, @authorkristinacowan.